I0119648

James Francis Corrigan

A history of the Phoenix park patriots

James Francis Corrigan

A history of the Phoenix park patriots

ISBN/EAN: 9783337306311

Printed in Europe, USA, Canada, Australia, Japan

Cover: Foto ©ninafisch / pixelio.de

More available books at **www.hansebooks.com**

A HISTORY

PHŒNIX PARK PATRIOTS.

BRADY.	FAGAN.
CURLEY.	KELLY.
CAFFREY.	POOLE.
O'DONNELL.	

The Brave Deeds for which they Died.

TRAITORS, MOCK-TRIALS, HANGINGS.

GOD SAVE IRELAND.

NEW YORK:

"NUMBER ONE" PUBLICATION-CO.,

P. O. Box 1486.

1884.

Entered, according to Act of Congress, in the year 1883,

By JAMES F. CORRIGAN,

In the Office of the Librarian of Congress, at Washington, D.C.

PREFACE.

For a burglar shot in the act of looting a house there is no public sympathy. The fact that he is unarmed or taken unawares is no mitigation of his offence or opprobrium to the man who shot him. The fine sentimentality of thieves might make a distinction between the shooting of an armed and an unarmed robber, but the broad common-sense of mankind, generally, would recognize under either condition a good riddance. Lord Frederick Cavendish and Under-Secretary Burke are hence officially mourned and regretted as the silenced exponents of a system of governmental plunder, not alone territorial, but reaching even to sacred fireside liberties. Now that the dramatic pathos of their sudden taking off—manufactured by a subsidized press—has passed out of memory and the bare skeleton of the fact remains, public opinion has been readjusted to an honest appreciation the deed, and the sober second thought of the exiled Irish and all free and liberty-loving peoples the wide world over justifies what but of late was heralded as a crime. A conservatism that denies the right of man to act, according to the best lights of his own conscience, is slavish, and the object of this little book is to record the deeds of the brave men who, in killing Cavendish and Burke, acted in obedience to their convictions and conscience, full in the satisfaction of doing a service to their native land. Surely, they cannot be taxed with undertaking the deed to seek the cheap approbation of an unthinking every-day populace, even at home, or in the wider theatre of the great outside world. To speak of them as they really were, and give the public an insight into their lives, is the object of this modest effort.

CONTENTS.

	PAGE
Preface.	3
Honor the Brave	7
England's Reign of Blood	10
"Liberty a Serious Game".	12
Betrayed for Gold and "Protection".	20
For "Removing" Tyrants	33
Joseph Brady	35
Daniel Curley	44
Michael Fagan	52
Thomas Caffrey	55
Timothy Kelly	57
James Fitzharris	61
Joseph Mullett	63
Andrews and Kinsella	65
Henry Rowles	67
John Dwyer	69
James Mullett and others	71
Joseph Poole	72
Patrick O'Donnell	85
The Packed Jury System	115
The Effect of the Executions	118

A HISTORY

OF THE

PHŒNIX PARK PATRIOTS.

HONOR THE BRAVE.

[Dedicated to Number One.]

HONOR the brave who battle still
  For Irish right in English lands ;
No rule except their quenchless will,
  No power save in their naked hands ;
Who waged by day and waged by night,
  In groups of three or bands of ten,
Our savage, undespairing fight
  Against two hundred thousand men.

No pomp of war their eyes to blind,
  No blare of music as they go,
With just such weapons as they find,
  In desperate onset on the foe.
They seize the pike, the torch, the scythe—
  Unequal contest—but what then ?
With steadfast eyes and spirits blithe
  They face two hundred thousand men.

The jails are yawning through the land,
    The scaffold's fatal click is heard,
But still moves on the scanty band,
    By jail and scaffold undeterred.
A moment's pause to wail the last
    Who fell in freedom's fight, and then,
With teeth firm set, and breathing fast,
    They face two hundred thousand men.

Obscure, unmarked, with none to praise
    Their fealty to a trampled land ;
Yet never knight in Arthur's days
    For desperate cause made firmer stand.
They wage no public war, 'tis true ;
    They strike and fly, and strike—what then ?
'Tis only thus these faithful few
    Can front two hundred thousand men.

You call them ignorant, rash and wild ;
    But who can tell how patriots feel
With centuries of torment piled
    Above the land to which they kneel ?
And who has made them what we find—
    Like tigers lurking in their den,
And breaking forth with fury blind
    To beard two hundred thousand men ?

Who made their lives so hard to bear
    They care not how their lives are lost ?
Their land a symbol of despair—
    A wreck on ruin's ocean tossed.
We, happier here, may carp and sneer,
    And judge them harshly—but what then ?
No gloves for those who have as foes
    To face two hundred thousand men.

HONOR THE BRAVE.

Honor the brave !   Let England rave
   Against them as a savage band ;
We know their foes, we know their woes,
   And hail them as a hero band.
With iron will they battle still,
   In groups of three or files of ten,
Nor care we by what savage skill
   They fight two hundred thousand men.

ENGLAND'S REIGN OF BLOOD.

MANY of the English officials in Ireland, during the year 1881, amused themselves, in their leisure hours, writing threatening letters. The Land League was then in its zenith, but its leaders did not possess sufficient perception to realize the concealed object of the so-called threatening missives. There were Irishmen, however, who saw through the diabolical scheme. Quietly they ascertained who were the writers of the threatening letters to Lord This and Lord That, which, from time to time, appeared in the public prints. They soon became satisfied that it was, at best, a bunglingly planned plot on which to form a new basis for establishing more coercion for the much coerced and starving Irish people. The Land League leaders realized the motives which had prompted the British officials to indict the warning letters when it was too late to thwart the object for which they had been penned. The plot was exposed when the cowardly and extraordinary orders given to the Ennis police were openly approved of and defended in the English House of Commons, on Wednesday, April 19th, 1882, by Forster, Chief Secretary for Ireland. The following is a copy of the police circular :

ENNIS, March 4, 1882.

" As there is good reason for the belief that every possible means will be used to assassinate Mr. C. Lloyd, it behooves the men (the policemen) of this county to be on the alert to prevent it. Men proceeding on his escort should be men of great determination as well as of steadiness, *and even on suspicion of an attempt should at once use their firearms* to prevent the *bare* possibility of an attempt on that gentleman's life. If men should *accidentally* commit an *error* in shooting any person *on suspicion* of the person being about to commit murder, I shall exonerate him by coming forward and producing this document.   H. SMITH,

" First County Inspector."

Similar instructions were given to the police of the other counties, and as a result, before a month had passed, the long-planned atrocities began. The record made by Drs. Macauley and Darling in May, 1882, told a terrible story of an affair, at which the Ballina police, "not even on suspicion," used their firearms on unarmed youths. There were other serious outrages committed by "Buckshot" Forster's orders, and while the red-coats and police were shooting down the people and crowding their dungeons with suspects, certain Land Leaguers were bartering with the tyrants.

The time for retaliation came at last, and an Irishman rallied his countrymen, not on the O'Connell doctrine, but on the sound principle of "an eye for an eye and a tooth for a tooth." These were the only principles the English really feared. Years before the London *Times* said :

"It is quite time that all the struggling nationalities should clearly understand that freemen have no sympathy with men who do nothing but howl and shriek in their fetters. Liberty is a serious game, to be played out, as the Greek told the Persian, with knives and hatchets, and not with drawled epigrams and soft petitions."

In Ireland, England and Scotland, about the period the so-called threatening letters were ascertained beyond doubt to have been written by one British official to another, there was formed a society of avengers, the Dublin branch of which is now known to history as the "Irish Invincibles." The society was founded by a man possessing, it may justly be said, as much courage and daring as William Putnam McCabe, of Antrim, or Michael Dwyer, of Wicklow, the famous revolutionary missionaries among the people of 1798. He was simply known as "Number One," and until he chooses to reveal his identity no true Irishman will venture to do it for him.

"LIBERTY A SERIOUS GAME."

UPON the resignation of "Buckshot" Forster, the British Government, in league with the so-called Irish leaders, and to deceive the people, appointed Lord Frederick Cavendish to fill the vacancy and carry out Gladstone's Irish policy of extermination.   When the new appointment was announced the royal Irish members of the British Parliament appeared well satisfied with it, and endeavored to make the oppressed believe that it was a victory, and that at last a brighter day had dawned for Ireland.   Thus ran the line of deceit ; but there were Irishmen who had carefully watched and considered every move made by the Britishers.   They understood the Castle compact as well as, if not better than, those that had actually formed it, and were prepared at the proper time to expose the plot.   Irish revolutionists, "and not of a low order either," deemed it necessary for their cause to remove the new Chief Secretary, and perfected their plans accordingly.

Under-Secretary Thomas Burke, an anti-Irishman, was for fifteen years the power behind the throne.   He was the real governor of Ireland, and for all the atrocities committed by Forster's orders he was alike responsible.   Forster was simply Burke's mouthpiece, and Cavendish was a new trumpet, so elegantly plated as to dazzle all that beheld it.   Saturday, May 6th, 1882, was the day selected for the installation of the new Chief Secretary by the Britishers, and for the removal of Lord Frederick Cavendish and Under-Secretary Burke by the Irish.   On the morning of that day Earl Spencer, in company with the new Chief Secretary, arrived in Dublin from England.   What was called the official entry took place at noon, and Lord Frederick Cavendish, under the protection of English troops, rode through the streets of the Irish capital in the train of the Lord Lieutenant.   An hour later Cavendish took the oath, swearing to do all in his power to trample out a noble race.   After the ceremony the Chief Secretary went to his apartment and remained there till six o'clock. He left the castle, and proceeded on foot to the Chief Secretary's lodge in Phœnix Park.

He knew the way well, for he had been there often when his brother, the Marquis of Hartington, was Chief Secretary. Half an hour later Burke left the castle and overtook Lord Frederick at the park gate. He got off the car, and both walked along the main road through the park. The new official was anxious to inspect his quarters before dining with Earl Spencer at the Viceregal lodge. The Lord Lieutenant had only a few minutes previously ridden out to the lodge with his attendants, and was walking in the garden when he observed a scuffle going on three hundred yards distant on the park road. He thought it was only a brawl, but gave directions that a policeman should be sent to see what was the matter. Little did he suppose that his brother tyrants were then being removed from office forever by patriotic Irishmen.

Arm in arm the old and the new British officials in Ireland strolled along one of the walks in Phœnix Park on their way to the Viceregal lodge. At a few minutes past seven o'clock they arrived at a point less than one hundred yards distant from the Phœnix monument. Just at that moment a hack drove along the road, from which several men alighted. A struggle followed. It was short, sharp and decisive. By it the removal was completed. Two men on tricycles passed along the road a few seconds before the scuffle occurred. They were named Foley and Maguire. After riding around for about ten minutes the tricyclists returned to the spot where the affair had taken place. What they discovered was best told by Foley. He said :

"When just opposite the Viceregal lodge we observed a man lying on the road on the right side and a man on the footway, about six or eight yards from us, lying on his back. I alighted from my tricycle and went to the man on the road and then to the man on the footway. I saw that the man on the footway had had his throat cut. My companion did not alight from his machine at all. He rode very hard to town, and informed the police. I went over to the man lying on the road and asked him a question to see if he had life. He merely turned his eyes. I could get no answer. Then I ran to the man on the footway and took hold of his left hand, which was lying across his heart, to feel if his pulse was beating.   He just gave his last breath, and blood oozed up from his neck.''

Colonel Forster recognized the body found on the road as that of Lord Frederick Cavendish and the one on the path as that of Under-Secretary Burke.   The bodies were removed by the police to an hospital.

The post-mortem examination at the Chief Secretary's lodge showed eleven wounds on Burke and eight on Cavendish.   The chief wound on the former penetrating the heart, and on the latter the chief wound severing an important artery in the neck.   One wound on Cavendish's left forearm had severed the muscles and fractured the bone, as if inflicted with a hatchet or sword.   The body of Burke presented the appearance of that of a stalwart man for his age —sixty years.   His face was drawn a good deal.   Cavendish was a man of slight build, with a narrow chest.   Burke's body presented —as a doctor stated who saw both bodies—very much the same appearance as that of Lord Leitrim.

The news of the removal of the brace of tyrants spread quickly throughout Ireland, and when Sunday dawned intelligence of it had reached America.   It then appeared that liberty was certainly a serious game, and was being played out for the first time in Irish history just as the Greek told the Persian, '' with knives, and hatchets, and not with drawled epigrams and soft petitions.''   The English officials in Ireland shivered in their boots, and the Hawkshaws of Scotland Yard were telegraphed for to assist the much-boasted-of Castle detectives.   They had theories.   One was that the avengers came over from England, and that Lord Frederick was deliberately the object of their attack ; and another that Burke, who was the chief instigator of Forster's policy and very obnoxious to the nationalists, was the primary victim.

Notwithstanding that the search by the detectives was a vigorous one, no progress was made.   They sought for a clew, but none could be found.   Forced to make some show for their money they, however, made three arrests of the '' corner-boy'' class at the village of Chapelizod.   These prisoners, according to the stories told by their captors, were unable to give a satisfactory account of themselves. A suspicious point gathered against them was that on Saturday night the trio had slept in the fields.

In the hope of capturing the avengers, a ludicrous circular, purporting to describe the Irishmen, was gotten up and distributed by the police. It ran as follows : " Wanted, for the murder of Lord Frederick Cavendish and Under-Secretary Burke, two men, the first, aged thirty-three years, stout, fair complexion, whiskers, short and dark, and mustache, wearing a blue pilot coat and soft hat ; the second, aged thirty years, hair, whiskers and mustache sandy, pale complexion, and dressed in a faded brown overcoat and soft hat. Both men had the appearance of sailors or firemen."

On the next day, Sunday, Earl Spencer, under guard of a strong force of royal dragoons, mustered up sufficient courage to leave the Viceregal lodge, and proceeded to the Castle to consult with the other frightened officials. He then looked pale and anxious. While there he appeared pleased at a copy of a Land League manifesto issued from the Westminster Palace Hotel, which had been penned by a friendly hand. It read :

To the People of Ireland : On the eve of what seemed a bright future for our country, that evil destiny which has apparently pursued us for centuries has struck at our hopes another blow which cannot be exaggerated in its disastrous consequences. In this hour of sorrowful gloom we venture to give expression to our profoundest sympathy with the people of Ireland in the calamity that has befallen our cause through this horrible deed, and with those who determined, at the last hour, that a policy of conciliation should supplant that of terrorism and national distrust. We earnestly hope that the attitude and action of the Irish people will show to the world that an assassination such as has startled us almost to the abandonment of hope of our country's future is deeply and religiously abhorrent to their every feeling and instinct. We appeal to you to show by every manner of expression that, amid the universal feeling of horror which the assassination has excited, no people feel so deep a detestation of its atrocity, or so deep a sympathy with those whose hearts

must be seared by it, as the nation upon whose prosperity and reviv-
ing hopes it may entail consequences more ruinous than those that
have fallen to the lot of unhappy Ireland during the present genera-
tion.   We feel that no act that has ever been perpetrated in our
country during the exciting struggles of the past fifty years has so
stained the name of hospitable Ireland as this cowardly and unpro-
voked assassination of a friendly stranger, and that until the murderers of Cavendish and Burke are brought to justice that stain will sully
our country's name.   CHARLES S. PARNELL,
                                           JOHN DILLON,
                                           MICHAEL DAVITT.

Communications of a similar nature were received by the British
officials in Ireland from a few men said to be leaders, but who were
in heart untrue to their country's cause.   With Parnell they denounced the brave Irishmen as assassins for striking what the London
Post, on the same day, declared to be " a blow aimed at English su-
premacy in Ireland."

The detectives still continued in pursuit of the removers, who, a
postal card had informed them, were *Irish Invincibles*.   They pro-
cured a " valuable" piece of evidence from an American who visited
Phœnix Park and scrutinized the footprints around the spot where
the Englishman and the anti-Irishman died.   He asserted that he
distinctly recognized marks of the peculiar broad-toed boot commonly
worn by Irish-Americans.

This theory indorsed the views of the *Pall Mall Gazette* on the
subject.   They were as follows :

" The American Fenians had made no secret of their designs.
There were special grounds for thinking that some piece of ferocity
on their part had been for some weeks close at hand.   The prospect
of the pacification of the country was calculated to disgust the extreme Fenians.   It is probable enough that they had drawn lots for
an attempt on the life of Forster, but had been baffled.   The change
in the policy of the government only made them more resolute in
their determination to establish a blood feud between Ireland and
England."

The Invincibles that the British detectives were so anxious to capt-
ure remained in Dublin, but members of another organization mys-
teriously vanished, much to the disgust of the puzzled and alleged
shrewd representatives of English law in Ireland.

Following closely in the wake of Dillon, Davitt, and Parnell, two
men, said to be Irish, misled by the bartering Land Leaguers, cabled
over to the Castle officials the following extraordinary message :

" A reward of $5000 (£1000) is hereby offered by the Irishmen
of Boston for the apprehension of the murderers, or any of them,
of Lord Frederick Cavendish and Mr. Burke on Saturday, May 6th.
On behalf of the Irishmen of Boston.

" JOHN BOYLE O'REILLY,
" PATRICK A. COLLINS."

Parnell and a few of his followers denounced the " removals"
until the following manifesto, posted on the walls of Dublin, informed them of the true character of the alleged " friendly
stranger."

"GOD SAVE IRELAND."

DUBLIN, May 8, 1882.

*To the Irish People and all Lovers of Liberty, and particularly our
brothers of the I. R. B. and kindred organizations :*

As there seems to be a grave misunderstanding as to the aim and
scope of the late executions at Dublin, we, the Executive of the
I. R. B., hereby request all the aforesaid to withhold their opinion
of this matter for the present, and to refrain from the expression of
sympathy at public meetings, which tend to humiliate Ireland, and
to give aid and comfort to England.

As to the monster Burke, he had preyed upon the lives and liberties of his countrymen for many years, and has deserved death a
thousand times at our hands ; and as to Lord Frederick Cavendish,
the lineal descendant of the infamous Lord Broghill, who hanged the
gallant and patriotic MacEagan, Bishop of Ross, at Carrigadrohid,
because he would not betray his country—his very name stinks in
the nostrils of the Irish people by the iniquities of his brother, Lord

Hartington, and the wholesale evictions of his father, the Duke of Devonshire, thereby driving thousands of the rightful owners of the soil to the poorhouse, exile and death.

This organization has tolerated the vagaries of Mr. Parnell and his *safe treason-mongers* until he has filled the bastiles in our country with the victims of a useless Parliamentary agitation, which left 20,000 persons homeless last year, and drove millions of the flower of our people to exile ; this ceases to be harmless when a truce is made by which he himself and his friends are allowed to go free ; and eighty (80) of Ireland's bravest sons are left to languish in prison, to be exiled or assassinated, and these the men who by the so-called " outrages" opened the prison doors to Mr. Parnell and his friends.

If England really wished to deal fairly by Ireland, why not issue a general amnesty, by which the prison doors would be opened and thousands of our exiled brethren, who now pine in foreign lands, could return in safety and honor ? Instead of this, Mr. Gladstone sent emissaries to the venerated head of the Catholic Church, who, by lies and false representations, have deprived thousands of our poor, persecuted people of the comforts of religion by turning our altars into political platforms.   Let us ask the people of Ireland, are there no classes of the people to be considered except the farmers, and of what avail will it be to Ireland if a selfish class is firmly rooted in the soil and becomes thoroughly loyal to England ?

We ask our friends in America to ponder on our desperate circumstances, to think of a brave and honorable people driven to despair by witnessing the white bosoms of our women torn open by the bayonets of English mercenaries, and our children of tender age shot down in the high-ways, while our wails of anguish are stifled in our blood.

We are convinced that no true prosperity can exist in Ireland so long as England possesses her custom-houses there, allowing her manufactures to pass into Ireland duty free, thereby leaving our Irish mechanics unemployed, and the enormous war tribute enacted by England taking away the produce of the land, thereby forcing the Irish people to starve.

Now, furthermore, we call upon all our brothers in America, particularly the advanced Nationalists, to aid, by every means within their power, the men who have carried out this execution, and we hereby further declare that they deserve well of their country. By order of the EXECUTIVE OF I. R. B.

BETRAYED FOR GOLD AND "PROTECTION."

So well had the executions of the tyrants, Burke and Cavendish, been carried out that never at any time were the Irish Invincibles in danger of falling into the hands of the alleged sleuth hounds of the British Government. They remained in Dublin, while search was being made for them in far more remote quarters. A man, at times named Welsh, and again Westgate, led the detectives a lively chase to Jamaica, only to disgust them by developing into a full-fledged "crank." British spies in America, anxious to get the large reward and the favors of a bloodthirsty government, were on the alert, all to no purpose. The offer of the reward for the betrayal of the removers was repeated, and large posters with "V. R." and other royal trash, were renewed on the bill-boards in front of the military and police barracks in England, Ireland and Scotland. Days, weeks and months passed, and, although during that time fully three hundred persons had been arrested, the Irish Invincibles had not been discovered. British detective ingenuity was puzzled when the arch-traitor, James Carey, and two or three other base wretches came to the rescue. They concluded to sacrifice the lives of their fellow-men to the murderers of their race for British gold and "protection." Then, and not until then, were the members of that fearless body of Irishmen, now known as the Irish Invincibles, revealed to the Castle horde. James Carey told all that he knew and a great deal more, and Robert Farrell, Myles Kavanagh and Joseph Smith, like him, were prepared to swear to anything and everything that would suit the government and place brave Irishmen on the gallows. They did so, and to-day those perfidious villains await the doom which their treachery deserves and which they cannot escape.

The traitors are under the alleged protection of the British Government, but by the removal of the much-despised rascal, Carey, the fact has been demonstrated that the discipline of the Irish Invincibles still remains intact, and no matter where the miserable informers may

be sent, they will find an Irishman ready and willing to perform his
duty to his country's cause, even if, in doing so, he has to sacrifice
his own life. The Irish Invincibles are not as small a body as was
sworn to by the traitors. They number thousands, hundreds of
thousands, yes, millions. Every Irishman, in fact, who has his
country's good at heart is an Invincible.

When Carey had completed negotiations at the Castle concerning
the betrayal of the Invincibles, which was in December, 1882, the
agreement was made that he and several others should be arrested as
"suspects" under Forster's Coercion Act, so as to allay suspicion.
The arrests were accordingly made, and while the traitors were in the
hands of the government all the plans were perfected for the conviction of a number of Invincibles—innocent or guilty, it mattered not
—for the killing of Burke and Cavendish.

On the night of the 11th and morning of January 12th, 1883,
twenty-one persons were arrested in Dublin and thrown into jail.
Among the number was James Carey, Town Councillor. Carey, when
first arraigned, remarked that "the conspiracy was on the bench."
Seventeen of the prisoners were secretly examined at a private investigation. Some of them signed depositions, others were not
asked to sign, and still others were not sworn. The plot was thus
made plain, and it was clear that the latter had been convicted before
being tried. Nine days later the men were arraigned in the Police
Court, and charged with conspiracy. Great discrimination was ex-
ercised by the police in the admission of citizens into the Green
Street Court room.

Few situations could be more impressive than that which was revealed when the prisoners had been placed at the dock and awaited
the advent of the first witness. The statement of Murphy, on the
part of the Crown, was an exceedingly brief one, and disclosed little
or nothing of the specific nature of the charge against the accused
beyond what was generally known in that regard. Neither those
who filled the body of the court nor the men in the dock had long
to wait, however, before something more concrete than was conveyed in the speech of the Crown counsel was developed. Robert
Farrell, the informer, was placed in the witness-box. As he was

sworn a smile and a look of amused incredulity passed between some
of the men in the dock. Farrell declared himself (upon his oath) to
be a laborer.

In the dock there was less excitement, less anxiety and, apparently, less concern than manifested itself among those who were spectators of what, regarded from whatever point of view, was a thrilling
scene. It cannot honestly be denied that seldom has a dock contained so large a number of intelligent-looking men. Patrick
Whelan stood in one end of the dock ; he took occasional notes, and
more than once exchanged glances with his wife, who was present
—glances which seemed intended to give to the woman's heart
some little portion of that courage and confidence in the issue which
it was patent to the most casual observer animated his own. Only
once did anything like a strong ebullition of temper glance from the
dock to the witness-box. When the informer detailed a conversation which he said took place touching the Chief Secretary, and
stated that Brady and another man were present during the colloquy,
Brady, clearing his throat and flushing with indignation, growled out
strenuously, " You're a liar !" with no small emphasis upon the epi-
thet. Not one of the prisoners—and they were representative of
almost all the stages of manhood—showed either trepidation or concern. Occasionally they smiled as some piece of "evidence" was
adduced or some remark from the professional men present touched
the chords of their risibility. The informer was pressed by the ex-
amining counsel as to whether he could recollect the substance of a
conversation which, he stated, had taken place in a certain public-
house between him and some of the men in the dock. He hesitated,
said that he could not " presently" recollect, and his answer to that
effect was being taken down when one of the counsel for the defence
said, *sotto voce*, " Exercise your imagination," and the dock took
the point, and a smile of good-humored raillery overspread every
prisoner's countenance—a smile seemingly more in keeping with any
other position than that in which they stood.

When what is known as the preliminary inquiry was begun,
Carey's programme was closely followed. Robert Farrell, the informer, first took the stand. He swore that nearly all the prisoners

were Irish Invincibles, and that several of them were present when he was asked to join the inner circle, formed for the removal of British officials in Ireland. He also deposed that Laurence Hanlon told him that he had taken part in the attempt to remove Juror Field ; that Joseph Brady stabbed Field, and that Timothy Kelly participated in the affair. The informer further swore that the Invincibles were picked men. He was followed by William Lamie and Myles Kavanagh.

James Carey, although the first traitor, was examined last. He sat in the witness-chair, his back toward the prisoners, his eyes on the ground, an inscrutable problem to all who strove to read him. He was dressed with considerable care, with a leaning to the style called " horsey ;" wore a yellowish tweed suit, and his boots had uppers of yellowish cloth. His face would require an astute physiognomist to interpret from it the full character he confessed to, the mouth and lower portion being covered by a thick and dark brown beard and mustache. Still it has features whose meaning is evident enough ; a low and receding forehead, brows constantly contracted and lowering, and eyes downcast, as if in continual meditation of some dark and terrible plot—the features of one " fit for treasons, stratagems and spoils," of a born conspirator of the criminal and unscrupulous type. He gave his evidence in a low and measured voice.

Carey identified the prisoners in the dock. They were : James Mullett, Joseph Brady, Henry Rowles, Thomas Martin, Timothy Kelly, Peter Carey, Edward McCaffrey, Edward O'Brien, Joseph Hanlon, Laurence Hanlon, Peter Doyle, William Moroney, Daniel Delany, Joseph Mullett, Daniel Curley, George Smith, Michael Fagan, Patrick Delany, James Fitzharris, Thomas Doyle, Thomas Caffrey, and Joseph Smith.

The examination of Carey was conducted by a lawyer named Murphy. His evidence was as follows :

Q. In 1861 or 1862 did you become a member of the Fenian Organization ? A. I did.

Q. From 1867 to 1868 what position did you occupy in the Fenian Organization ? A. I was always a member of the Dublin Directory.

Q. Did you know of there being in the organization those who constituted a Supreme Council ?　A. No, I never knew.

Q. Did you ever try any person by court-martial ?　A. Several.

Q. Up to this time—in 1879, or so—what class of persons solely used you to try by court-martial ?　A. Informers only.

Q. Did Edward McCaffrey bring any man to your house in November, '81 ?　A. He did.　A man who passed by the name of Mr. Walsh.

Q. Did this man, Walsh, tell you what the object of his visit to Dublin was ?　A. Yes.　The establishment of the Invincibles.

Q. Did he tell you whether or not any names had been submitted to him ?　A. Yes, four.

Q. Where had those names been submitted to him, did he say !　A. In London.

Q. When McCaffrey left you alone with Walsh, what did Walsh do ?　A. He asked me was I willing to join the society, and when I told him I was he then produced the terms, with some writing on paper.

Q. Did he administer an oath or put any words to you ?　A. He repeated some words off the writing while I held a knife in my right hand.

Q. Go on with the words as well as you can recollect them ?　A. " With my own free will, without any mental reservation whatsoever, I will obey all the orders transmitted to me by the Irish Invincibles ; nor to seek more than what is necessary for carrying out of such orders, the violation of which shall be death."　There were more words than that, but I forgot them.

Q. In a few days after that did Walsh come to your house again ?　A. He did, accompanied by Mullett, Edward McCaffrey and Daniel Curley.

Q. Did he tell you what these three were to do in Dublin ?　A. He did.　We were to be the four in Dublin.

Q. Did he tell you what were to be the numbers of the Irish Invincibles in England, Ireland or Scotland ?　A. About two hundred ; not to exceed two hundred and fifty over the kingdom.

Q. Did he tell you out of what society or organization these men were to be selected ? A. Out of the Fenian Organization. All picked men. [Loud laughter in the dock.]

Q. How many were to be selected ? A. Not to exceed fifty.

A prisoner—Town Councillor Carey.

Q. Did Walsh, in the presence of the other three and you, tell you what was to be the immediate object of the society ? A. He did. To remove all tyrants from the country. [Laughter.]

Q. Did he then give you the names on the list of the society that were to be removed ? A. He did.

Q. What names did he tell you ; were the names returned by the London society ? A. Forster, Earl Cowper and Burke.

Q. Did you come subsequently to know a man named P. J. Sheridan, of Tubbercurry ? A. I never knew him.

Q. And was that the man you were afterward told was P. J. Sheridan ? A. It was.

Q. What was his disguise ? A. The Rev. Father Murphy—[Carey laughing at Lawyer Murphy]—a namesake of yours.

Q. Did Walsh tell him who you were and where you had been ! A. He said, " We were out in the Park, looking out to see Forster, to make his acquaintance."

Q. Did you know a man named Captain McCafferty ? A. I do. (After a long pause.)

Q. Was it after Walsh had left that McCafferty had called on you ! A. Yes. He called at my place twice. On the first occasion he gave me twenty-five pounds in gold and on the second fifteen sovereigns. I did not know him then as Captain McCafferty.

Q. Who told you that he was ? Edward McCafferty ? A. I believe he was a man that had been once tried here. I believe he was imprisoned.

Q. To whom did you suggest knives ? A. To Sheridan. Not knives but daggers. McCafferty gave directions about putting cord round the handles.

Q. After Sheridan left you at the hotel and went over to London, did Frank Byrne's wife bring over any weapon to you ? A. A woman came with them. She brought a rifle, two revolvers, and about six knives,

Q. After McCafferty had left you, do you recollect any other man coming to visit you ? A. I do.

Q. Did you ever come to know his name ? A. Never.

Q. Did you ever see how he used to sign his name ? A. If he left a note for me he would sign himself " Number One."

Q. Did he often meet with Mullett, Curley, McCafferty and your-self ? A. He did very often. If not at my house, at McCafferty's, 21 Peter Street.

Q. When this man " Number One" wanted to see you to whom used he send the message ? A. Generally he came to my place.

Q. Do you recollect the occasion on which a man named McMahon was shot in Dorset Street with a revolver ? A. On the Monday be-fore that day arrangements were made to remove Forster.

Q. Where was the attack to be made on him ? A. The corner of Victoria Bridge.

Q. Who was next to you in station along the line ? A. Stephens.

Q. And who was next to him ? A. Harry Rowles.

Q. And who were the persons who had assembled near where the attack was to be made ? A. I saw them afterward.

Q. Was that when you came down yourself ? A. I saw McMahon, Joe Brady, Tim Kelly, Daniel Curley, Leonard and another man, who is outside. The man who was charged and arrested with Brennan.

Q. Where, at Westland Row ? A. Between that and the Castle—Sunday, Monday, Tuesday and Wednesday ; four nights.

Q. On Monday where were you searching for him ? A. At the mail boat in the evening.

Q. And Tuesday ? Morning and evening, and Wednesday, until Thursday night. A. We adjourned after the mail boat went, and then came back at nine o'clock for the last train.

Q. On Tuesday were you there for the mail boat again ? A. I watched him that evening. I met him in Dame Street ; my arm touched his ; he was accompanied by a tall young gentleman ; they went into the post-office on College Green at five minutes to six o'clock—the telegraph office.

Q. Were you at Mark's Church at six ? A. I was and waited for a few minutes.

Q. Were any of the members of your society (the Invincibles) there at any time that evening ? A. I met them afterward.

Q. What did Daniel Curley tell you that they did ? A. He said that they had looked for Forster—that his carriage came, but that he went out some other way. If he had not he would not be alive to-day.

Q. From whom did you ascertain that Forster was not to come back after that evening ? A. From " Number One."

Q. Was he in the town and in communication with you during the time that nearly all these attempts were being made ? A. Nearly always. He was there that Wednesday night.

Q. I ask you if that man ever divulged his name ? A. Never.

Q. When he told you that Mr. Forster was not to return again, were you told by him to whom you were to direct your attention then ? A. Yes. To Burke. The four of us arranged to get the car. We arranged everything ourselves.

Q. Were you in the Park on the 5th of May ? A. I was. I went there in a cab from my own door at 10.30 A.M.

Q. Who went with you ? A. Only the driver, Fitzharris.

Q. Did you meet any person opposite the Vice-Regal ? A. Yes. " Number One."

Q. Was your Chairman Curley with you ? A. He was, and Joe Brady, and Patrick Delany, and Caffrey.

Q. What kind of a man was " Number One" ? A. He was a respectable-looking man.

Q. Did he tell you anything about his position ? A. Oh, no ; but I inferred by his military remarks that he was a military man.

Q. He gave you money ? A. Eighty pounds and said there was no limit. He said, " If you required a thousand pounds you could have it."

Q. Where did you believe it came from ? A. I said I did not think from America. I think I expressed myself, but I know between the four of us it was repeatedly said, "Perhaps they are get-

ting it from the Land League." Some of them suggested that, and
some said, " Perhaps from America."

Q. When you started on this organization of the Invincibles you
had no communication with respect to it with the Directors and other
members of the Fenian Brotherhood ?   A. None whatever.

Q. So far as you saw, was it totally independent and outside of
it ?   A. Yes.

Q. Did " Number One" on the 4th or 5th of May say anything
about the delay in removing Burke or any of the days before up to
the 5th ?   A. Burke was not mentioned until the 3d.

Q. What did he then say ?   A. He said we would go for Burke.

Q. Do you recollect seeing the car coming down that Curley said
he would send back for you ?   A. Yes ; Kavanagh was driving it.

Q. Where did Kavanagh pull up ?   A. Opposite the seat where I
was.   He turned the horse facing the road, with the seat to the pathway, and proceeded to feed him.

Q. Before you got on the car did you see any one coming ?   A.
Yes, two ; they were together.

Q. In what direction did you go ?   A. On straight toward the
Phœnix.

Q. On your way up on the car had you a handkerchief in your
hand ?   A. I had.   A white one.

Q. Was that the prearranged signal ?   A. It was.

Q. Did you pass Fitzharris's cab before you stopped ?   A. Yes ;
that was on the right-hand side.

Q. Could you give the names of the seven you saw there ?   A. I
can.   Joe Brady, Tim Kelly, Pat Delaney, Thomas Caffrey, Michael
Fagan, Daniel Curley, Joseph Hanlon—that is the seven.   Of course
they knew what was coming.   They saw the handkerchief.

Q. Who had control of the arrangements ?   A. Daniel Curley.
Brady and Curley came over to me on the car, and I leaped off, and
he said, " Is he coming ?"   " Yes," I said.

Q. You said yes ?   A. Yes ; I said, " Yes, the man in the gray
suit.   Mind, be sure—the man in the gray suit."   I started then on
the angle along the road, and the two gentlemen were not two hundred yards away from me.

Q. And, after they had passed, did you see anything done to one of these men ? A. Carey (amid dead silence) said—When I was about two hundred and fifty yards away from the place where I left those men—I looked around occasionally before that—but at that distance I looked and I saw the seven men meet the two. The first three were abreast—Curley, Fagan and Hanlon ; twelve feet after them Kelly and Brady, and six feet Delaney and Caffrey. I saw the two meeting the seven, and the two passed through the ranks. They let them pass through. I said "It is another failure." I went on a few steps farther and I looked around. I saw a right-about move- ment made by the first four. I went on a few steps farther and I looked again, and I saw the two men in the rear getting to the front and closing on the two first men—the two gentlemen. What I saw then I will describe. I saw one figure coming in collision with the two gentlemen. The man in gray was on the inside ; I did not know the other. I saw this man, Joseph Brady, raising his left hand and striking the man in the gray suit. That is all I saw.

Q. What gate of the Park did you then make for ? A. The Island Bridge gate. It was seventeen minutes past seven o'clock when I was leaving the men ; the whole transaction was over by twenty minutes past seven. When I left the pathway I looked at my watch.

Q. Was Curley at your house that night ? A. He was ; about half-past eight. I was not there. I met him about nine o'clock at night, at the corner of Holles Street.

Q. Did he tell you what they had done to the two men ? A. He did. I asked him : "Is it true what I hear, that Lord Frederick Cavendish and Burke were both killed ?" " I believe so," said he ; " of course, I don't know whether they are killed or not," said he.

Q. What did he say he had seen ? A. What did he say he had seen ? He said when he had seen the two parties pass through the four, and two men turn quite round about, he thought there was going to be another failure. These three men were armed with re- volvers.

Q. State what Curley described was done ? A. " I saw then that they closed upon the two gentlemen, and I saw," he said, " Joe Brady attacking one gentleman, and following the other out in the road and attacking him also. I saw him coming back from him to the other party, and then I saw him wiping the knife in the grass to take the blood off. I stood still until I saw them all on the car and the car drove away.''

Q. Did he tell you what way they drove in the cab ? A. He said they drove down straight to the Gough statue. The man on the velocipede went driving down after them. He was covered with the revolvers by the men in the cab, and they turned the corner toward Phibsborough. The cab turned toward the Constabulary Barracks.

The Clerk—The cab, you say, turned up toward Phibsborough ? A. They got out there, and went to the *Express* office, and put a card in under the letter-box, stating how it was done. Curley did.

Q. The newspaper office ? A. Yes, and the Irish *Times* next day and the *Freeman.*

Q. By whom did they say it was done ? A. On the card was written, '' Executed by order of the Irish Invincibles.''

Q. Do you recollect, after that, Curley and Brady and you meeting in Ned Caffrey's house ? A. Yes, the following night. '' Number One'' was there also.

Q. What occurred between you on that night ? A. We got the history complete from Joe Brady in the presence of the strange man. The knives were produced at the next meeting which took place a week or ten days afterward.

Q. Who produced them ? A. Joe Brady.

Q. Did this man—this superior officer—give directions as to what was to be done with them ? A. Yes—to have them destroyed. I thought bad of destroying them. I wanted to send them to the exhibition.

Q. How were they destroyed ? A. Broken up in little pieces and the handles burned and the dust produced.

Q. When had you the last interview with this man called '' Number One'' ? A. About a week after the excitement—about the end of September or October 1st.

Q. Where had you the interview with him ? A. At Blackrock Station.

Q. He wanted you to account for the finding of certain articles ?

A. That's the business I had with him. I told him that I knew nothing at all about it. I thought that Rinkle gave information, and went away to America. I went myself, and could not find them, and that is all I know about it.

Q. Did you resign at any time the position you occupied as one of the four that had charge of Dublin and the Invincible Society ? A. I did, in the end of June.

Q. To whom ? A. To "Number One."

Q. You have mentioned in your evidence that you wished to have certain knives sent to the exhibition ? A. Yes, I did.

Q. May I ask why ? A. Just the way that they would be preserved.

Q. As a public curiosity ? A. As a national relic, or any way you like to put it.

Carey—I never got any one arrested. I want to save my own and other people's innocent lives.

Q. Have you a brother in the dock at the present moment ? A. I have.

Q. And you are no informer ? Certainly not. [Laughter from the dock.]

Thomas Caffrey—You are a double-dyed informer.

After Carey's deposition was read he corrected it in several particulars and modified the statement concerning Mrs. Byrne by saying that he had only been told she was the wife of Frank Byrne. He also corrected the statement that James Mullett was in his company when he and Curley met "Number One." Counsel for the prisoners objected to the alterations, saying that Carey had discovered from the newspapers that Mullett was in prison at the time of the alleged meeting. The magistrate allowed the objection and the deposition was ordered to stand so as to show the discrepancy.

The police court proceedings which had taken over two weeks were brought to a close on the 19th of February. On that day the prisoners were committed for trial to answer the charge of murdering Lord Frederick Cavendish and Burke. The prisoners committed for trial included all that were under examination, except Patrick Whelan, who had been liberated on bail. After the prisoners had been committed the Crown counsel stated that Joseph Smith would be examined at the trial. The Crown counsel, after the committal of the prisoners, said that it was with great reluctance that the Crown had accepted the evidence of a prisoner, who might have been the director and instigator of the tragedy. It had been done, however, in the interest of public safety and for the public good. He trusted that the Executive had thereby obtained the power to perfectly penetrate this, fearful organization, and he hoped to make amenable to justice the plotters as well as the perpetrators of the murder. He also stated that he hoped to be able to produce the man known as " Number One."

A number of paid witnesses were also examined during the inquiry. Their evidence was manufactured and they perjured themselves to please the cowardly scoundrels in whose pay they were. Although Carey swore that the knives found in the house in South Cumberland Street were not the ones used by the patriots, a Dr. Myles deposed that some of the wounds of Lord Frederick Cavendish and of Mr. Burke were just such as would have been inflicted by the knives produced. And Cameron, the City Analyst, deposed to some stains of mammalian blood on one of the knives.

FOR "REMOVING" TYRANTS.

AFTER mature deliberation on the part of the Dublin Grand Jury they found "true" bills against the Irish Invincibles on the 9th of April. Joseph Brady, Timothy Kelly, Patrick Delaney, Thomas Caffrey, and James Fitzharris, also known as "Skin the Goat," were accused of having participated in the Phœnix Park removals. Joseph and Lawrence Hanlon, William Maroney, Michael Fagan, and Joseph Mullett were also indicted for having done their duty to their country. They were conveyed from Kilmainham Prison to the Green Street Court-House at nine o'clock that morning. The government felt rather afraid that friends of the prisoners would attempt their rescue, suspicious-looking men, believed to be Americans, having been seen in Phœnix Park and other parts of Dublin for several days.

The court-house was besieged by crowds of persons eager to gain admission. The authorities, however, only admitted the jurors called in the case and fifty reporters, and they were let into the building at an early hour. "Justice" O'Brien took his seat on the bench at fifteen minutes past eleven o'clock, when the work of swearing in the Grand Jury was proceeded with. Mallon, the chief of the detectives, and a few privileged spectators were also present. The prisoners were escorted by a whole troop of dragoons.

When what was called the trial began, "Justice" O'Brien informed the Grand Jury that the case of the attack upon Juror Dennis Field would not be brought to their notice until after the ordinary business of the commission had been disposed of. Addressing the special jurors, he spoke at some length of the importance and gravity of the Phœnix Park case. He pointed to the existence of regularly organized secret societies drawn and held together for the purpose of committing murder. Those members of such societies who were actually guilty of taking the lives of their fellow-beings and those who were guilty of assisting and encouraging them in their deeds, were clearly guilty. The latter were equally guilty with the former. He dwelt on the affair which had, as if by magic, brought a dark cloud over the "bright and favorable prospect that, it had seemed, was about to open for Ireland."

He had not, for his part, the least misgiving that the jury would be found faithful in the discharge of their onerous duties. The Grand Jury then retired, but soon returned to the court-room with a true bill against Joe Brady, charging him with the murder of Lord Frederick Cavendish and Burke. Brady was arraigned at the bar and pleaded not guilty.

An application was then made for the postponement of the trial, as the preparations for it were not complete. The counsel for the Crown opposed any longer postponement than next day. Mr. McCune, Brady's solicitor, said that Mr. A. M. Sullivan would act for Brady if time was allowed him to get ready. O'Brien said that the case must proceed next day. If Mr. Sullivan was not ready to take it in hand he ("Justice" O'Brien) would appoint some other person to act for Brady. The case was further considered, the result being that the trial of Brady was set down for the following day, and Dr. Webb Adams was assigned by the court to defend the prisoner. Curley, Kelly, Thomas Caffrey, and Fitzharris were each arraigned separately. They each pleaded not guilty. All were held for trial. Brady, when placed in the dock, wore as careless and defiant a demeanor as he did at the hearing.

JOSEPH BRADY.

WHEN Joseph Brady was called to the bar on the morning of the 10th, the alleged trial was postponed for twenty-four hours. Dr. Webb Adams, who was assigned to act as counsel for the brave Invincible, declined to conduct the defence, giving as his reason that he was not prepared. Another lawyer named Sullivan was then directed by the bench to assist him. Brady was again placed in the dock on the 11th, when the farce of trial at the Green Street Court-House began. Notwithstanding the fact that it was known that all absentees would be summarily fined one hundred pounds, many of the jurors on the panel failed to appear and respond to their names. The work of swearing in the jury occupied one hour, the counsel for the prisoner having the right to challenge twenty of the number.

The case for the Crown was opened by a Mr. Porter. He pointed out to the packed jury that the duty they were called upon to perform was one of the most serious that could fall on citizens. Porter described the crime as one of unparalleled atrocity—a crime that had shocked the whole civilized world. He declared that the object of the conspiracy was to remove all whom they regarded as tyrants, probably with the ultimate purpose of forming a republic, of which the four original leaders—Mullett, McCaffrey, Curley, and Carey— would be the leading spirits. He referred to Sheridan's share in the removals as his undertaking to provide arms when there should be a call for them. Brady and men of his class, he said, were among those who were always prepared for murder; but they were without doubt entirely indifferent as to the ultimate objects of that murder. Brady was at hand when the various ambushes were laid for Forster.

The counsel for defence here interposed an earnest protest against the Crown counsel being suffered by the court to prejudice the jury against the prisoner Brady by making assertions like these which could not be proved.

The Judge, however, refused to interfere.

The first witness called was Farrell, the informer.   During the examination of Farrell counsel for the prisoner again protested against
the introduction of matters foreign to the present charge and relating
only to the attempts made against the life of Forster.   " Justice"
O'Brien said that only such evidence was admissible in the present
case as tended to connect the prisoner with the conspiracy.   Farrell's
evidence went to show that Brady was associated with the members
of the Inner Circle, and that he was secretary to Curley.

James Carey was the next witness.   His evidence was the same as
he had before given.   Upon the conclusion of Carey's direct examination, the court adjourned for the day.   Carey's face was flushed
while he was giving his evidence.   Carey was in the witness-box for
an hour and three quarters.   Carey became perfectly cool in his
demeanor toward the close of his evidence.   One of the knives found
in Ringend Basin was produced in order that he might identify it as
one of those supplied by Sheridan from London.

On the second day of the hearing Carey was again placed on the
witness stand and was cross-examined by counsel for the defence.
Carey said that he was promised a pardon before he determined to
give evidence against his fellow-conspirators.

The answers of the witness to questions put him concerning prom-
ises of pardon were given with much hesitation.

Finally he said that he had been informed by Mallon, Chief of
Detectives, that if his evidence should be given freely to the State
and should be confirmed by that of other witnesses, he and his brother
would be pardoned for their share in the conspiracy.

Myles Kavanagh, who drove the car in which the Invincibles
rode, was then called to the stand.   He repeated his former evidence
in substantially the same language.   He made a material amendment
to it, however, by saying that it was Smith, not Delancy, whom he
drove to the scene of the removals with Carey.   His statement made
before was a mistake.

Joseph Smith, another informer, repeated the story of his doings
in Phœnix Park on May 6th, as related by James Carey at the preliminary hearing.   Smith said he was sworn in as an Invincible three
weeks before the removals were committed.   The Invincibles had a

secret sign by which they recognized each other, which was the holding of a knife in the palm of the hand. Daniel Curley had intro-
duced himself to witness by means of this sign.

Counsel for the defence spoke for an hour. His argument was in
support of an alibi for the prisoner. Counsel denounced Carey's
villainy in having betrayed men whom he had seduced into the
commission of crime. The informers, he said, had contradicted
each other on important points. The rule was infamous that an informer's testimony, unaccompanied by any other evidence, should
be accepted. Interested evidence must be corroborated by disin-
terested testimony. In this case such evidence was lacking.

Annie Meagher deposed that she was with Brady, at her uncle's
home, on the 6th of May, at five o'clock in the afternoon, and again
from a quarter to seven until eight o'clock in the evening.

A keeper of a public house, named Little, was the next witness.
He deposed that Brady was in his house at four o'clock in the afternoon, and again at a quarter to nine o'clock in the evening, on the 6th
of May. The cross-examination, however, elicited the fact that
Little's house was the regular rendezvous for the Invincibles.

As Brady was conveyed back to prison there were hisses for
Carey and cheers for Brady. The demonstration was so marked that
the police arrested two of the offenders.

On the third day of the trial a clerk named Kennedy was placed
on the stand. He swore that he spoke to Brady, who was accompanied by a girl, on Dominick Street, between five and seven o'clock
on the evening of May 6th last, the date of the Phœnix Park removals. He recognized Annie Meagher, who testified that she was
with Brady on that evening, as the girl in question. Witness said
he also met Brady on the following day. Upon the conclusion of
Kennedy's testimony the defence announced that they would call no
other witnesses.

Dr. Webb, counsel for the prisoner, said he begged to submit his
respectful protest against any evidence being allowed in this case
which would bear upon the existence of a conspiracy prior to May
3d, even though evidence were excluded by that means which
would throw light on a plot existing before that date to remove

Burke. The only exception to this principle would be that evidence
which concerned the words and acts of the prisoner might with pro-
priety and according to the rules of evidence be admitted. In support of his position he cited various authorities, running from the
time of Edward I. down to the present. He said : " The prisoners
were first arraigned on the charge of conspiracy ; this was followed
up by the more serious charge of murder. I contend that such a
combination of charges is unprecedented in the history of criminal
cases."

The Court here interposed, reminding Dr. Webb that the present
indictment was not one of conspiracy and murder, but the single indictment of murder.

Dr. Webb, continuing, said : " An indictment for conspiracy to
murder, your Honor, may only be based upon evidence going to
show that there was a design to murder some definite person." He
declared that the law regulating the evidence of aiders and abettors
in cases of conspiracy could not be made to apply in the present
case.

Mr. Adams, closing the defence, said : " Heaven forbid that I
should ever be arraigned before the tribunal of public opinion as the
defendant Brady has been, in advance of the regular trial. Brady's
case has been prejudged ; his guilt has been presumed in a manner
the most scandalous on record. Let not the jury be led away and
prevented from doing justice because the crime is awful in its nature,
but let them consider solely the question whether Brady is guilty.
Let them bear in mind that the chief evidence against him comes
from persons who spoke to save their own necks. Such evidence
must be regarded with great suspicion."

Naish, for the Crown, in his reply said that the circumstances of
the crime are not doubted ; it is equally conceded that it was the
fruit of a conspiracy and was not a matter of personal revenge.

The speeches closed, " Justice" O'Brien, charging the jury, said
Carey had every conceivable motive and inducement to give in his
evidence statements calculated to serve his own purpose ; he had told
a straightforward story, and one which did not spare himself. The
jury were exhorted to consider, however, that if he had been de-

tected in swearing falsely, the Crown would be justified in proceeding against him the same as against the other prisoners. The same general rule was applicable to all the informers. In making up their verdict they should set aside all prejudice, all the weakness that frequently influences our judgment and biases our words. He expressed the hope that they would be influenced by Divine inspiration. The jury then retired.

There was a rustle and movement in court as the jury rose from their seats. Joe Brady was taken away from the gaze of the crowded court to the down-stairs apartment reserved for prisoners, and the anxious and eager expectation of all who witnessed this last terrible scene could not prevent the half-hour interval while the jury were absent from being devoted to the hum and buzz of conversation throughout the court. The Judge had retreated to his own private room behind the bench directly at the conclusion of his charge. The jury went out at eleven minutes past three, and then came a long and weary time of expectation. From the door at the back of the gallery the foreman of the jury was seen descending, followed by his colleagues, to take his seat. Without delay the Judge was summoned, and the prisoner was brought up from below.

Very slowly the jury passed into their box, looking, every one of them, pale and burdened with the weight of the awful responsibility resting upon them. Then came the solemn words, "Are you agreed upon your verdict? Do you find the prisoner, Joseph Brady, guilty or not guilty?" In a scarcely audible voice the foreman said the word "Guilty," and the clerk of the Crown repeated it once more to make sure. Joe Brady was not overcome by the verdict. The Judge directed the clerk to ask the usual formal question of the prisoner whether he had any reason to allege why sentence of death should not be passed upon him.

Joe Brady's reply was characteristic. "I am not guilty," he half hissed, half shouted out, with a strong Irish accent and with a voice husky with passion. "I am not guilty of the charge," he shouted again, and savagely denounced the "paid informers," who had sworn falsely against him.

The sentence was then pronounced. It was that on the 14th day

of May next, Joseph Brady be hanged by the neck till dead.   After
the sentence had been pronounced, Brady, who meantime had recovered his composure, rose in his seat and with solemn vehemence protested his innocence of the crime.   After making his last disclaimer
he was hurried from the court-room by the Britishers.

Joseph Brady remained a close prisoner from the moment of his
conviction until the moment he became an Irish martyr.   He was
visited by his mother on the evening before his execution.   She was
heard to exclaim, "Mind, Joe ; no statement."   Brady smiled, and
replied, "Don't be foolish ; do you think I am a fool ?"

May 14th, the day on which Joe Brady died at the hands of the
Britishers, was Whit-Monday.   It was a day of mourning throughout Ireland, and in consequence the usual festivities were abandoned.
The stores in the Irish metropolis were kept closed during the whole
of the day.   It was a quiet way the people took to let the foreigners
know that they sympathized with the Invincibles.   The morning
opened beautifully, but as it wore on there were occasional showers.

Fully ten thousand persons, consisting principally of young men of
the artisan and shopkeeping classes, gathered on the roadway surrounding Kilmainham prison as early as half past six o'clock, waiting anxiously for the hoisting of the black flag, which was to indicate
to the outer world the fall of the drop.

There could be no doubt about the sympathies of the masses.
There was no levity, no rude horse-play.   People talked in whispers
commiserating the man who was about to die.   As the clock struck
eight the cord was tightened around the neck of the unfortunate
man within the jail, and before the last stroke the death emblem was
fluttering in the breeze.   A loud murmur ran through the crowd ;
hats were off in an instant ; many went down on their knees in the
roadway, and others devoutly crossed themselves and uttered prayers
for the repose of Brady's soul.   The sun, a few moments afterward,
shone out in summer splendor, and in less than half an hour the large
crowd had dispersed.

Brady retired early to rest on Sunday night, and rose at four next
morning.   He was rather depressed for about an hour, but he soon
recovered his usual spirits.   After writing a letter to his mother, in

which he bade her farewell and asked her to pray earnestly for him, he partook of a small breakfast, and shortly before seven accompanied Canon Kennedy and Father O'Reilly to the chapel, where he confessed to his spiritual director and received the last rites of the Church. At seven minutes to eight the doomed man and his spiritual advisers left the chapel. In the hall outside Marwood was waiting with the officials who were to take part in the melancholy procession to the scaffold. Brady submitted quietly to the process of pinioning. Holding a prayer-book in his right hand, he earnestly repeated the responses. The distance to the foot of the scaffold was traversed slowly.

At the foot of the scaffold Brady turned to the warden and said, "Take the book." He never uttered another word, but slowly, deliberately, without apparent falter, mounted the eight steps leading to the drop, Canon Kennedy keeping by his side, and Marwood with the leg straps in his hand. A moment more and he stood on the fatal plank. Only when Marwood went to place the noose round his neck did he flinch. He jerked his head suddenly to one side, but recovered himself in a second. Exactly on the stroke of eight Marwood touched the lever. Death was instantaneous, the vertebræ of the neck being literally smashed to pieces. The length of the drop being eight feet eleven inches, the effect of this on the neck of a man who weighed fourteen stone can easily be imagined.

The body, after hanging the legal hour, was cut down and laid on a rude bench beside the small scaffold, to await the post-mortem view of the jury. It was attired in the clothes in which Brady was arrested—small round jacket, dark trousers, vest, and woollen shirt. The inquest was held in a small arched room close to the yard in which the scaffold was erected. The coffin was ready, and the jury had no sooner given their verdict than the remains of the brave Irishman were placed in the grave, dug not far from the scaffold. The only evidence at the inquest was that of the doctor and the chief warder.

Marwood, in a brief interview with a reporter, stated that he never hanged a man who gave him less trouble or anxiety, or displayed calmer or more unflinching front.

A juryman stated that the features of the dead man were slightly swollen and his eyes protruded. His tongue was half cut in two between his teeth.

A wreath of flowers was received by Brady, to which was attached a card bearing an expression of grief at his fate, from Irishmen living in Liverpool. Brady made no statement to the jail chaplain or to the governor of the prison.

The heartlessness with which the English Vandals treated the aged parents of the young patriot was told in the columns of the Dublin *Irishman.* Concerning an occurrence that took place on the day of the hanging, it said : " But what words can be applied to the act of the government officials, two police inspectors, who, at the very moment that Brady was standing upon the scaffold, burst into his father's house, and, disregarding the anguish of the grief-stricken family, proceeded to ransack the premises ? Their reason was, they explained, that they suspected that a coffin was concealed in the house. A mock funeral was to take place, they thought, and they had orders to prevent it. It is useless to search the records of the worst despotisms of Europe for anything approaching this incident in cold atrocity. A parallel can only be found in the history of Ireland, and one has not far to seek to discover it."

And the *Irishman* adds : " At the farewell which took place between Joe Brady and his mother on the Saturday before the execution, the afflicted woman was denied the consolation of a last embrace ; she would not be allowed to touch the son whom she had nurtured to manhood. By a special ' kindness ' she was ultimately permitted to shake hands with him, warders standing between."

Even the Sisters of Mercy would not be allowed to visit the doomed man to prepare him for death, unless in the presence of three warders. The holy ladies would not submit to such an outrage upon their sacred character, and it was only on the day before the execution that the three-warder condition was relaxed. If the Government could pursue the soul of Brady before the Throne of the Most High, their officials would do so.

The attention of all Irishmen desirous of striking a blow is called to the following list : Richard D. King, No. 9 Mount Street Cres-

cent, insurance agent (foreman) ; Walter Brown, No. 1 Hanover
Square, East, miller ; Robert Bowles, Nos. 23 and 24 Wellington
Quay, printer ; John D. Grattan, No. 18 Merrion Street, Upper,
draper ; Joseph H. Byrne, Casino, Malahide, gentleman ; Bernard
McGrath, No. 17 Fownes Street, wholesale merchant ; William
Dowse, No. 16 Mount Street, Lower, builder ; Thomas Butler, Jor-
danstown, Oldtown, farmer ; William A. Hayes, Nos. 45 and 49
New Row, Poddle, tanner ; James Dobson, No. 114 Stephen's
Green, West, house painter ; Thomas James Bowers, No. 212
Great Brunswick Street, gentleman ; William Hynes, No. 28 Elgin
Road, gentleman.

They were the tools of the tyrants that sent Joe Brady to an early
grave. May the vengeance that their act deserves fall on them !

DANIEL CURLEY.

DANIEL CURLEY, the second prisoner, was arraigned on the 16th of April. The evidence of the informers, Carey, Kavanagh, Farrell, and Smith, was simply a repetition of that given in Brady's case. Their examination occupied a day and a half. Then Dr. Webb opened the case for the defence. He compared James Carey to Titus Oates, who, like Carey, was induced to swear away the lives of innocent men in similar circumstances by a similar system of lavish rewards. Continuing, he said this plot was a plot with one conspirator, and that conspirator was James Carey. He said he was prepared to clearly establish the innocence of Curley by proving an alibi.

The first witness called by the defence was Peter Hanlon, father-in-law of Curley and uncle cf Joseph and Lawrence Hanlon, two of the conspiracy prisoners awaiting trial. He swore that Curley was in his company from six to eleven o'clock on the evening of May 6th, between which hours the murders occurred.

A plumber named Hopkins was the next witness. He said he saw Curley standing on the outside of a saloon at a quarter to seven o'clock on the evening of May 6th. The barkeeper of the saloon swore that he served Curley at six o'clock that evening.

Mr. Adams, counsel for the prisoner, spoke for the defence. Referring to the evidence against Curley given by Kavanagh, the car-driver, Mr. Adams declared that it did not prove that Curley was in Phœnix Park on the 6th of May. His presence there, said Mr. Adams, was indicated by the testimony of James Carey, who had stated that Curley was in command of the Invincibles at the time of the removals, but Carey swore to that effect in order to save his own neck from the gallows. There was no doubt that Carey himself was in command.

Porter, Attorney-General for Ireland, replied on behalf of the Crown. He declared that the evidence offered by the defence in support of an alibi for Curley was worthless and conflicting.

After he had concluded his argument the Judge delivered his charge to the jury. His remarks were strongly against the reliability of the evidence to prove an alibi. He pointed out that there could not be the slightest doubt that the murders were perpetrated at the instigation of secret societies with which the prisoner was indisputably connected. The charge was completed at half-past two o'clock, and the jury retired immediately. They were absent but a short time, and on their return to the court-room announced that they found Curley guilty as charged in the indictment.

Clerk of the Crown.—Daniel Curley, you have here been indicted, that you, on May 6th, 1882, feloniously and of malice aforethought, did kill and murder Thomas Henry Burke. To that indictment you have pleaded not guilty, and put yourself on your God and your country, and a jury of your countrymen have found you guilty. What have you now to say why sentence of death should not be passed on you?

The Prisoner.—I will say distinctly that I am not guilty of the charge I am accused of. I had some remarks to make, but it was not until I heard your lordship's charge that I determined to say this —that it is a biased, unreasonable charge.

"Justice" O'Brien.—Daniel Curley—

The Prisoner.—You will excuse me, my lord, if I say a few words. Since the proceedings commenced I pictured all to myself with reference to identifications made after the imprisonment and the acts of the informers. At the time I was identified all the parties were prepared to identify me. There were twelve or fourteen of us brought into the yard, and I was on the extreme left, and then I was ordered to come and stand in the centre of the line. On another occasion a warden was ordered to stand at the rear of the man—Joe Mullett— for identification. These are the points that are unreasonable. These are the points that I have spoken to counsel on. There are several other matters that I would wish to remark upon ; but there are other people awaiting their trials, and, of course, to meet the same fate—I expect—not that I fear death ; I never courted it ; I deny the charge ; I say between myself and God this minute that the two men who identified me as being at the polo ground—no, I never

was there. I was not near the place. I was not in the Park on May
5th. You will have to be very cautious, my lord, about the
informers. I don't seek redress. Of course, I expect no mercy.
I don't pray for pardon. I expect none from the British Government ; they are my avowed enemies. Peter Carey, for instance. I
know the position in which I am standing here. I am standing on
the brink of the grave. I will speak the truth. I never spoke to
him about Kavanagh or any one else. He certainly saw me in his
brother's house ; but a word I never spoke to him about Kavanagh.
There is a lot of the evidence that my humble ability is not able to
analyze nor my memory able to recall at the present time. As to
that Emma Jones, she did not see me in the Park that evening, nor
yet did I ever speak to Carey. You said that I would have had time
to come from Burke's to the Park with the whiskey in my pocket.
You analyzed carefully all the evidence given in my behalf, and you
pointed out all the defects of it carefully and minutely, and you
repudiated the evidence to a certain extent ; but, on the other hand,
when you were pointing out the evidence of the informers, you just
put them all together and said, " If you don't believe them, don't find
the prisoner guilty. ;'' but you do not point out their contradictions,
as far as myself and these informers are concerned. I admit I was
sworn into the Fenian organization twelve years ago, when I was only
twenty-two years of age, and from that time to the present I worked
openly in the organization. I was let into a number of their secrets,
and I say here to-day that I will bring them to my grave faithfully
and truly ; and, as to my own life, if I had a thousand lives to lose
I would lose them sooner than bring to my grave the name of an
informer, and that I should save my life by betraying my fellow-man.
No finger of scorn shall be pointed to my character, morally or otherwise. And as to the whiskey, I was not drinking whiskey that night ;
it was port wine I was drinking for months. My wife was not in the
habit of drinking, either. You may take my life, but don't take my
character, nor my wife's either. But James Carey—ah, if he was
telling the truth ; but he is not, and Joe Smith is not telling the
truth. My lord, I had nothing to do with them. There is another
point that has come to my memory. How James Carey turned

informer. There are many gentlemen in court at the present time, as well as the prisoners up at Kilmainham, who know that previous to his turning informer he told my fellow-prisoners that I turned informer. Then, I suppose, when he heard that I turned informer, he said to himself, "I will nail Curley, anyhow." Such is the case. I told the governor the circumstances—that he made use of those expressions ; and I am certain that this is the reason he is so bitter on me. And when, of course, Mr. Smith comes up—a man whom you will have to be very cautious with. Nevertheless, of course, as I said before, he will have to meet his God—so will I. We know who is the most truthful. Mr. Smith then came up. According to his own evidence in that chair, what did he say ? The very moment he was arrested that he gave information in the matter truly. Did he say that he knew me ? No, he did not know me. He was put into the yard to exercise with me for three weeks. I observed his attitude. Every time he would have to retire he would get into a position in the exercise-yard where he would have a full view of my face. If he was walking before me he would look back ; he would go behind me when I turned a corner. I said to myself naturally, "I expect this fellow is up for something," which I saw afterward that he was. I have tested him. There are many things, as I said before, that I have to say ; but, knowing that prisoners are to be tried after me, and fearing through my ignorance in speaking over general topics that I might get them into a hobble on technical points, that's simply the reason I will abstain from saying more.

"Justice" O'Brien here assumed the black cap.

The Prisoner.—My lord—

"Justice" O'Brien.—You have been already heard. The sentence of the Court is that you, Daniel Curley, be taken from the bar of this court to her Majesty's prison at Kilmainham, and on May 18th be taken to the place of common execution, and be there hanged by the neck until you are dead ; and may God have mercy on your soul.

The Prisoner.—My lord—

"Justice" O'Brien.—Remove the prisoner.

The Prisoner.—I have to thank my counsel here—

(The prisoner then turned to leave the dock, and exclaimed, as he descended the steps, " God save Ireland !")

. Daniel Curley, it was asserted, was one of the leaders of the Irish Invincibles. He was also said to have been chairman of the executive four of the Dublin branch of that organization. It was he who was supposed to have dropped the cards into the letter-boxes on the night of the removal of the tyrants. They were directed to several newspapers, and on them was written : " Executed by order of the Invincibles."

Again, at a few seconds before eight o'clock, on May 18th, the black flag proclaimed to thousands gathered round Kilmainham Jail that another member of the Invincible Society had been strangled to death by the Britishers.

The morning broke with all the splendor of a summer day. Groups of men, and many women, before six o'clock took up positions from which a view could be commanded of the dismal signal.

On the night before his execution Curley retired to rest about ten o'clock, but before doing so he wrote a letter to his wife and children. It read as follows :

" MY DEAR AND EVER-BELOVED WIFE AND CHILDREN : I take this opportunity, the last on this deceitful earth, of saying a few words to you, hoping you will forgive me for the step I took with regard to my trial—I mean for not trying to save myself as others did. But I could not stoop so low, or bring myself to do so. My dear wife, I will die as I have lived, faithful to my principles and to my country's cause. I will do as all honest men do—bring my secret to the grave with me, and leave them that are at freedom to enjoy it. Dear wife, I will say no more on this subject, as I have domestic business to speak of. I will request of you to keep a vigilant watch over our dear children. Keep them to their school and religion and off the street, as you yourself know that I dread to see children getting the run of the street. Dear Jane, do not think, because I say this, that I have not confidence in you. I have the greatest confidence in you. Yes, dear wife, I will die at rest, for I know you will do what is just to them. I will also request of you not to let them out of your sight or care to any one as long as you can help it.

"My dear and faithful wife, now about yourself. As I have told you before, I will not ask to restrict you in any manner. If you think it well to change your widowed life, you can do so with all my wish and blessing. I never like to see any one tied. I love liberty. But, my dear wife, if you ever change your life, be very careful in your choice in a companion against deceitful men. Oh! my dear and faithful wife, I hope you will excuse me if I cannot speak of this matter, as it was very hard to tear my truthful heart from you and offer it to God. And what a trial that a base and brutal deceiver should be the cause of separating two loving and truthful hearts ; but God's will be done. That is my only consolation. My dear wife, I will ask of you to be attentive to your religious duties. No matter how much you are engaged in the business of the world, never neglect them. My reason for saying so is in order that I shall meet you in the kingdom of heaven, never to be parted by the power of men. My dear wife, I am sure you will be glad to hear I die in peace with all men and forgiving my enemies. May God forgive them for the injury they have done me. I am happy and at peace with God. Oh! may God protect you and my dear children in this deceitful world. Remember me to your dear father, mother, Frank, Peter, Nelly, Mr. and Mrs. Hiland, granny, Misey, and all friends. Believe me to be your faithful and loving husband.

"DANIEL CURLEY.

"To his affectionate and faithful wife and dear children—Mary, Jane, Michael, Peter, and Daniel. Pray for the soul of your dear husband and father. May the Lord have mercy on my soul."

Then follow a number of crosses, signifying kisses.

The crowd outside the prison was as large as at Brady's execution. There were more women. The black flag went up at half a minute to eight o'clock. A wail rose from the people and the "Hail Marys" were repeated with greater rapidity. Nearly all uncovered their heads, and many women burst into tears. The saddest scene was witnessed behind a small confectioner's shop by the Inchicore Road, where Curley's father and father-in-law, both old men, were walking up and down bareheaded. As the flag ran up to the staff the old men gave vent to their grief in loud wails and threw themselves on their knees. After praying for some time with fervency they began " keening." Their piercing cries attracted the attention of the crowd, which rushed from all points to ascertain the cause of the noise. The impression spread that some one had fallen over the bridge which at this point spans the river. The poor old men re-mained on their knees for an hour after the execution. Curley died firmly. Curley retired to rest at twelve o'clock, and rose that morning at six, looking calm and refreshed. At a quarter to seven Canon Kennedy and the Rev. Mr. Findlater arrived and took him to the chapel, where he partook of the last sacraments. An hour was spent there. Mgr. Kennedy then told Curley to arise, and he at once obeyed.

The procession then formed in the same manner as at the execu-tion of Brady. On their way through the corridor Marwood joined the party, putting up his hand to his head as a salute. The priests took their places behind Curley, and the litany of the dying was re-cited, Curley repeating the responses in an audible, firm voice. He wore a crucifix around his neck. About ten paces from the scaffold Marwood made a signal to halt and then proceeded to pinion Curley, whispering something in his ear. Curley offered not the slightest resistance, and when the painful operation was over he stood erect and firm. Just before his arms were caught in the straps he stretched forth his right hand and shook hands with Governor Gildea, saying, " Good-by, and thank you." The recitation of the litany was then resumed, Curley repeating the responses with intense fervency. At the foot of the scaffold he took a last glance at those present to wit-ness his execution, and then ascended the steps of the scaffold lightly.

Indeed, he almost ran up. Then Marwood came quickly to his side and strapped his legs. He then adjusted his head, and, lifting it slightly, placed it within the noose, at the same time pulling the white cap over his face as the clock was striking eight. Marwood moved quickly to the side of the scaffold. There was a touch of the

lever and a sharp swish as the body descended through the trap, and Daniel Curley was dead. The length of the drop was nine feet, and death was instantaneous. Curley evidently died without pain, for the features were quite placid. The body was cut down at nine o'clóck, but the inquest was not held till ten. The usual verdict, death by hanging, was returned.

MICHAEL FAGAN.

"A FENIAN he lived, and a Fenian he would die," were the firm principles of Michael Fagan, who was called for trial on April 25th. He was also charged with removing Burke. Fagan pleaded not guilty. Messrs. Adams and J. O'Byrne were assigned by the Court to defend him. Great difficulty was experienced in forming a jury. Seventy-five of the persons called failed to make their appearance, and were fined £100 each. James Carey, the informer, was called to the stand, and testified that he had arranged to stab ex-Secretary Forster after the plot to shoot him had failed. He declared that he wished to remove tyrants, and he believed it was no sin to kill Burke. Joseph Smith, the informer, swore that Edward McCaffrey was in Phœnix Park on the evening of May 6th. James Carey, however, denied that he saw McCaffrey there on that occasion. Counsel for the defence regard the conflict between the two statements as important. The prosecution closed their case, and the case for the defence was opened.

An alibi was proved by witnesses. "Justice" O'Brien charged the jury. His remarks were to the effect that the testimony given by informers against the prisoner had been fully confirmed by that of other witnesses. The Judge having finished his charge, the jury retired. After a short deliberation they returned and announced that they had found a verdict of guilty against the prisoner. On being asked if he had anything to say why sentence should not be passed upon him, Fagan protested his innocence. He declared that "he was a Fenian, and would die one." The Judge then sentenced him to be hanged on the 28th day of May.

On that day Michael Fagan was as firm an Irishman as he was on the day on which he had been sentenced. He did not falter a step, but ascended the scaffold and awaited the executioner. The prison was surrounded by his countrymen and women, who, upon the hoisting of the black flag, repeated the Litany for the Dead.

The morning was cold and disagreeable, and rain began to fall a quarter of an hour before the expected signal was run up. Neither was the crowd demonstrative. Fagan's mother, brother, and sister were walking about in an aimless way, making no parade of their grief, and attracting little or no attention. The old woman, who comes from the neighborhood of Mullingar, had, it appears, sent a letter to the Queen asking for her son's life, but she was badly advised in taking a course which could only excite false hopes. From the first there was no hope of reprieve. A strange silence fell on the people as the monster hand of the clock travelled slowly round to eight o'clock. At that hour the dismal death token fluttered on the flagstaff, and a scene like that which took place on the two previous executions followed. All uncovered their heads, and many went down on their knees and prayed all the louder as the rain fell faster.

Fagan retired early to rest the night before, and rose at a quarter past six. At twenty minutes to seven Rev. Canon Kennedy and Rev. Father O'Reilly were in attendance on the doomed man, who was quite resigned and even cheerful in demeanor. He went with them to the chapel, where the last sacraments were administered. Meantime Marwood, who had affixed the rope with a drop of nine feet early in the morning, went out when he saw the rain, and placed a thick white cloth carefully over the rope to keep it quite dry. Fagan was quite firm, and walked steadily to the gallows, repeating in an audible voice the responses to the Litany for the Dying. He held a small crucifix in his hand, and retained it at the spot where Marwood pinioned his hands. Fagan submitted quietly to the operation, displaying just a shade of anxiety in his rapid step to get speedily to his doom. He made no statement, merely nodding to the priests and saying "Good-by" as he followed Marwood up the steps leading to the drop. In an instant Fagan was dead. The face became rapidly discolored, the blood trickling from the nose when, two minutes after the drop, Dr. Carte raised the white cap to look at the strangled man's face.

At nine o'clock the body was taken down and laid on the same bench on which the forms of Brady and Curley had been stretched for the inspection of the jurymen who had been impanelled to hold the usual inquest. An eye-witness stated that it would have been almost impossible to guess that Fagan was the doomed man as he walked quietly along with downcast eyes, intent on his religious duties and the responses.   The crucifix, which he held in his left hand, was retained firmly in his grasp, being removed only after the body had been taken down.   As the drop fell the white cap flew up on account of the rush of air caused by the descent of the body.   The face, as seen by those looking on, was calm, but slightly congested, and the skin of the neck was torn by the rope.   There was not the slightest struggle or quiver.

THOMAS CAFFREY.

THE motives which prompted Thomas Caffrey to act as he did were probably because he had become satisfied that the jury in his case would be a packed one. He stood in the dock on May 2d, and when asked to plead to the indictment filed against him, with a smile replied, "Guilty."

The consequence of pleading guilty was explained to him, but he persisted in his plea. On being asked whether he had anything to say why sentence should not be passed upon him, Caffrey replied in a loud, clear voice, "All I have got to say, standing on the brink of the grave, is, that I did not know what was going to happen until twenty minutes before the removals were committed. I was bound to go to the Park under pain of death." The Judge in passing sentence said there were no means of judging the truth of the prisoner's statement. He did not decide that it was necessarily wholly untrue.

Just one month from that day, June 2d, Caffrey was hanged. Although he saved the Crown the trouble of a trial, the Britishers made a distinction between his case and that of Patrick Delaney, who also pleaded guilty, and whose sentence was commuted. Delaney gave information which led to the conviction of Fagan, while Caffrey gave none. Besides, the Crown believed Delaney's story that he intentionally refrained from shooting Judge Lawson.

Caffrey expressed great contrition in parting with his mother and brother. He slept soundly the night before his execution, and rose at six next morning. At half-past seven he was attended by Jail Chaplains Canon Kennedy and Rev. Father Fennelly.

As the hour of execution drew nigh the crowd outside increased, several thousand having assembled. Caffrey's brother Larry and his wife were present, and wept bitterly. All the spectators were congregated on the bridge to watch for the black flag. At ten minutes to eight, as the prison minute-bell tolled, the procession was formed.

Caffrey walked with Canon Kennedy on the right and the Chief Warden on his left.

The Litany for the Dying was then recited, Caffrey joining with great fervor. In one minute and ten seconds from the time Caffrey set foot on the first step of the scaffold the bolt was drawn. Death was instantaneous, the drop being nine feet. The face was somewhat congested and the neck slightly excoriated by the rope. At the inquest, held an hour after the execution, the usual verdict was returned.

In his last interview with the condemned man, Larry Caffrey, holding the doomed man's son, aged four, in his arms, said, " Do not give the government any information ; do not satisfy them." The Invincible merely smiled and said, " Never mind that." His last words were to ask his neighbors to forgive him. In Caffrey's mother's house there is said to be a portrait of " Number One."

Caffrey's mother received from him a letter, of which the following in an extract : " Dear mother, I write you these few lines, for the last time in this world, and hope you will offer up all your sorrows along with my sufferings for my omissions in my past life. I hope you will forgive all who have done me harm in this world, as I forgive them from the bottom of my heart, as I expect to get forgiveness from my merciful Father in heaven. Tell all inquiring friends that I hope no one will ever throw a slur on my child or any one belonging to me for the death I am about to suffer, and I hope you will never have cause to blush when my name is spoken."

TIMOTHY KELLY.

THE boy patriot, Timothy Kelly, was the next of the Invincibles the British Government was anxious to send to the gallows. He was innocent, but the Britishers were satisfied that he was guilty, and that was enough. From the moment of his arrest the brave boy was doomed ; but notwithstanding the packed juries, there was considerable trouble before he was finally convicted. The young Invincible was placed in the dock on April 19th.

Carey was the main witness. For the defence Kelly's brother was the first witness. He testified in support of the claim of an alibi. that he was in the company of the prisoner on the 6th of May, at the time the killing occurred. The defence called four friends of Kelly, all of whom swore unbrokenly that the prisoner was in their company at the time Lord Frederick Cavendish and Burke were slain. One of the witnesses called by the defence to prove an alibi testified that he went to Phœnix Park with Kelly on Sunday, May 7th (the day after the removals), and that both of them made an examination of the blood-stains on the ground. The jury, after remaining out some little time, returned to the court-room and announced that they were unable to agree, and were discharged. Three days after, Kelly's second trial began. The alibi was re-proved, and in addition a man named Glyn, who identified Carey at the inquiry in Kilmainham Court-House as a man whom he saw in Phœnix Park on May 6th, testified that he saw four men in the park on the evening of that day, but Kelly was not one of them. Mr. Charles McGowan, who some years ago contested a seat in the House of Commons for the County Leitrim, was also called as a witness for Kelly. His evidence also went to prove an alibi. Altogether fifteen witnesses testified in favor of the prisoner's claim of an alibi. The Judge, in summing up the next day, nevertheless, spoke most strongly and warmly against the prisoner's claim of an alibi, arguing the case against Kelly. The jury, after being out a short time, returned to court and announced that they had been unable to agree on a verdict. They were rather tartly sent back to reconsider their verdict, but, after returning to the court-room the fourth time and reporting that they could not agree, were discharged by the Judge, who seemed much chagrined at his ill-luck.

In violation of the usual rules of criminal law, to give a prisoner the benefit of the doubts, Earl Spencer was determined a third time to put the testimony of Carey, the informer, against that of sixteen other witnesses and prove them to be perjurers. The jury panel was very carefully scanned, and a third trial of Kelly was begun on the 7th of May. A few days later James Carey, the informer, on being called to the witness stand swore, in addition to what he had before sworn, that Kelly had offered to turn informer. Carey said that he was the last man who offered to testify against the prisoners. Joseph Hanlon, another informer, confirmed the evidence given by Carey and Kavanagh, to the effect that Kelly was one of the four men who rode on Kavanagh's car on the evening of the Phœnix Park removals. The jury deliberated for an hour before they brought in their verdict of guilty. The Judge sentenced the prisoner to be hanged. On being removed from the dock, Kelly said, in a most fervent and sincere manner : "I am innocent." He also expressed his thanks to his counsel for their exertions in his behalf, and said he hoped they might live long to defend the innocent.

While the boy was patiently awaiting death, a petition asking for his pardon was forwarded to the "good old lady," which she treated with silent scorn. Timothy Kelly was the last of the Irish Invincibles sentenced to death for the removing of Messrs. Cavendish and Burke. Although it was not proven at any of his trials, it was asserted that he was the person that struck Burke, the monster, down. It was also said that Brady had told Carey that when he turned round after attending to Lord Frederick Cavendish, he found "Tim working away at Burke." Farrell swore that after the tyrants had been properly set the rest was left to Brady and Tim Kelly. June

9th was the day set for the hanging, and the boy patriot met death courageously.

Kelly's extreme youth—he was only nineteen—and boyish appearance, together with the fact that two juries disagreed before the Crown could get a verdict against him, attracted a large amount of popular sympathy.

At the parting interview between Kelly and his relatives, his father, mother, two brothers, and two sisters formed the visiting group. The father and one of the brothers are invalids, and they were completely prostrated after their final interview with their doomed relative. Mrs. Kelly was allowed to take flowers to her son, and in return got a lock of his hair, some religious books which he had been perusing, and other souvenirs. She said he was ready to die as a martyr for his country.

At twenty minutes to seven, on the morning of execution, Canon Kennedy and Father O'Reilly entered the cell of Kelly, who had been up and dressed since half past five o'clock. Mass was then celebrated, and the procession was formed to the scaffold precisely as at the other executions.

Kelly never flinched nor hesitated, but merely glanced at the rope dangling from the chain which secures it to the band encircling the beam. He prayed fervently, crucifix in hand. Marwood adjusted his feet in the pencil marks on the drop. Then, with a glance to see that the nine feet slack was quite clear, the hangman touched the lever, and Kelly met with instant death.

He left no statement of any kind, and expressed no wish to do so.

From an early hour there were more than fifteen hundred persons standing on the left-hand side of Island Bridge road. Prominent among them was Mr. Varian, of Sherrard Street, who formerly acted as president of the Prisoners' Aid Society.

Mr. Varian moved about with the official letter in his hand, asking those who might be supposed to know if there was any hope. No one could afford the slightest chance of hope.

Before eight o'clock the assemblage outside the jail increased to two thousand.

The spectators were much calmer than on previous occasions. Most of them uncovered their heads, and a few knelt down. One woman, evidently laboring under an attack of hysteria, knelt down and passionately called for " the curse of God on James Carey."

She presented a very shocking appearance, and her friends quickly dragged her away into a neighboring house.

JAMES FITZHARRIS.

THE car-driver, James Fitzharris, otherwise known as " Skin the Goat," was accused of having taken part in the removals of Cavendish and Burke, on April 30th. He pleaded not guilty. The case for the prosecution was opened by Porter, Attorney-General. He argued that although Fitzharris did not personally stab Burke, yet he was cognizant of the act and was an implement of the murder, as he drove off the assassins. No witnesses were called by the defence. The evidence against Fitzharris was given by informers. Mr. McInerney opened the argument for the defence. His address was eloquent. He dwelt on the fact that the accusation that the prisoner was in the Park with a knowledge of the errand of the removals, rested on the evidence of informers alone. He particularly pointed out that although Peter Carey swore that the prisoner had recounted the circumstances of the removals to him, his narrative of the executions had differed from ascertained facts. He closed with a pathetic appeal to the jury to restore the poor man to his starving family with a good name, which was his sole possession. The Judge, in charging the jury, pointed out that no evidence had been adduced to show that the prisoner was aware of the plot against Burke before May 5th. The earlier meetings which he had attended, the Judge said, were held to plot against the life of ex-Secretary Forster, and, therefore, had no connection with the charge. The fact was clear that Fitzharris was in the Park when the murders occurred, but if the jury doubted that he was guilty of knowledge of the mission of the men he drove, they were bound to acquit him. After the verdict of acquittal had been rendered, Fitzharris was taken back to jail to await trial on a charge of conspiracy to murder.

There was much rejoicing in Dublin at the failure of the Britishers to convict poor " Skin the Goat" on the same testimony that had sent other good men to the gallows. He was again brought to the bar on the 15th of May, and after a brief trial was found guilty by a packed jury. '' Judge'' O'Brien, in passing sentence, said : '' The crime of which you were convicted is morally the same as that of murder. The deaths of Lord Frederick Cavendish and Mr. Burke were mainly owing to your act in inducing Smith to point out the victims.''

Fitzharris was sentenced to penal servitude for life.

JOSEPH MULLETT.

For the attempted removal of Juror Dennis Field, Joseph Mullett was indicted on May 3d, and was called upon to reply to the charge seven days later. He refused to plead to the indictment, giving as his reason that the comments of the English press had served to prejudice his case. He also refused the assistance of counsel assigned to him by the Court. His trial then, by order of the Court, was proceeded with.

Porter, Attorney-General, in opening the case for the Crown, said that Mullett was charged with planning the attack on Field, and not with personally sharing in it. He stated that he would prove that the prisoner was a leading member of a conspiracy which, though it confined its operations to Dublin, had ramifications throughout the whole country. Porter read extracts from a diary kept by Mullett. One of the entries was an account for arms. The name of Arthur Forrester was attached to it. Forrester was supposed to be a leading Fenian. His wife and mother were witnesses to support the claim of an alibi on the trial of Fagan. A further entry said the government were foolish to bother about the Parnell procession, as the Parnellites were harmless. Porter read a letter from James Mullett, the brother of the prisoner, ordering the latter to make an example of a member of the Emmet band, who, the former said, had turned traitor. Porter commented on the entries in the diary. He said a book noting the cash received and expended had been found in Mullett's bedroom. It would prove that money had been given by (" Number One") to James Carey for the purposes of the conspiracy. Other papers found in the prisoner's room contained entries of money received, with initials attached, indicating that it came from Daniel Curley, Joe Brady, Arthur Forrester, Joseph Smith, and Patrick Delaney. Porter read an extract from Mullett's diary, entered September 9th, 1881, in which he implored the assistance of God for a special undertaking. In an entry made September 10th he said he had failed in the undertaking because two of his confederates had deserted him. This, Porter said, is supposed to refer to the abortive attempt on the life of ex-Secretary Forster. Farrell, the informer, testified that the prisoner gave orders to Hanlon previous to the attack on Juror Field.

Mullett did not call any witnesses. Addressing the jury in his own defence, he repeated that his case had been prejudiced by leading articles in newspapers and by speeches of ministers and ex-ministers. He was proceeding to mention the name of Sir William Harcourt, the Home Secretary, when the judge interposed. Mullett then refused to continue his address. The Judge charged the jury, and they retired. A verdict of guilty was rendered against Mullett. He was sentenced to penal servitude for life. After sentence had been pronounced, Mullett said : " I might as well be in prison at hard labor as anywhere else."

ANDREWS AND KINSELLA.

A YOUNG man whose name was supposed to be McMahon, but which proved to be Peter Andrews, died from a pistol-shot wound received at No. 6 Tighe Street, Dublin, during the month of March, 1883. Matthew Kinsella, a companion of the unfortunate youth, was arrested for the shooting, and although the discharge of the pistol was purely accidental, he was sentenced by the Britishers to twenty years' penal servitude. It was generally supposed that Andrews and Kinsella were Irish Invincibles, but the Castle detectives, unable to establish that fact, contented themselves with circulating a story to the effect that Andrews was killed because he was suspected of being an informer. The following letters which were published in a Dublin newspaper show the falsity of the base insinuations cast on the character of Andrews by the vile Castle hacks :

" SIR : As the afflicted father of the late Peter Andrews, who met his end at No. 6 Tighe Street, in this city, in March last, by a gunshot wound in head by Matthew Kinsella, who is now undergoing twenty years' penal servitude, may I hope that you will please to insert the following statement, which I have recently received by letter from Kinsella, dated from Mountjoy Prison, which will throw light as to how my unfortunate son met his untimely end ? It was alleged that my son was an informer, which induced Kinsella to shoot him ; but a perusal of his letter will show to the contrary, and thus dispel from the public mind that opinion. The following is a true copy of the letter which is in my possession.

Your obedient servant,   EDWARD ANDREWS.

"MOUNTJOY PRISON, Jan. 31, 1883.
" *To Mr. Edward Andrews, No. 46 Coombe Street :*
" MY DEAR SIR : I wish to say a few words to you regarding your poor son's death, and to assure you, as I would on my death-

bed, that he had met with his death by a pure accident, and not otherwise, hoping you do not believe it was otherwise—God forbid it was.　On that sad night when we met, he came with me home to remove from my room the fatal revolver, and when handling it in the room, when going to clean the rust off it—it was loaded, which I did not know—and, taking it up, I gave it a sudden turn by accident, when, to my horror, it exploded, and for some time I could not say in what direction it went.　Peter was sitting on a chair, and he never moved out of the posture in which he was till he attracted my atten-tion by not speaking.　I took hold of him by the hand, and asked him was he frightened, when he made me no answer.　I need not say the shock I got.　I examined him, and could see no mark on him.　I took him down-stairs, thinking he would come to, but when I brought him to the street I found he was helpless altogether.　I was going to convey him then to Stevens's Hospital, but by the light of a street lamp I saw he was bleeding fast, and knew he was then dead.　I need not say how foolishly I acted afterward.　I intended to explain the case to you the next day, but I was prevented.　I could not then even tell my counsellors, for if I did I would not be here this day.　May his soul rest in peace.

" MATTHEW KINSELLA."

HENRY ROWLES.

HENRY ROWLES was arrested on suspicion of being an "Invincible" and cast into prison. He was a married man and had resided with his wife and family at No. 11 Fishamble Street, Dublin. Carey swore that he was the man that had failed to give, near Kings Bridge, the signal on the occasion of the alleged designed attack on Forster. On that evidence alone the honest and industrious tradesman was consigned to a dungeon where he was treated by brutal keepers worse than if he was a mad dog. An indictment of "conspiracy to murder" was found against him. Rowles who had been in good health during the earlier part of his imprisonment, on Wednesday, March 14th, 1883, while at exercise in Kilmainham Jail yard, was taken with faintness, followed by a fit, and at once removed to hospital. Here he received treatment from Dr. Carte, and apparently recovered. On Thursday he got up and went down to the hospital yard and took exercise, but on that night, about ten o'clock, he was again attacked by fits, which, with short intervals, continued until his death, which, after a series of attacks, took place at seven o'clock Sunday evening, March 18th. Although unable to speak, deceased was, it is believed, sensible to the last, but it is also stated he made no sign or declaration with reference to the charge against him. He was attended daily by Dr. Carte. On Saturday Dr. Little was called in, and Dr. Cahill (stated to be his usual medical attendant) was summoned. The facts of his illness and decease were made known to his family.

The deceased, who was about forty-five years old, was of medium height and slightly pock-marked. The remains of the unfortunate prisoner, who was tortured to death in jail, were removed to his late residence. On March 21st, the body of the brave "suspect" was interred in Glasnevin Cemetery.

The funeral procession, which consisted of forty carriages and other vehicles, with a large number of people on foot, proceeded up

Thomas Street, and James's Gate to Stephen's Lane, down which it passed to the North line of quays. The route then taken was along the quays to O'Connell Bridge, up Sackwille Street, Rutland Square, Frederick Street, Blessington Street, and thence to the cemetery. On reaching the cemetery the remains were conveyed to the Mortuary Chapel, where the burial service was performed by the Rev. Walter Hurley. The coffin was then taken to the family burial place of the deceased in the St. Brigid's section of the grounds. The "Miserere" was chanted after the coffin had been lowered into the grave. The widow of the deceased and her large family of eight children were present. A considerable proportion of those who attended the funeral were women, among them being Mrs. James Mullett and Mrs. Edward McCaffrey. The coffin was of polished oak, richly mounted. The top of the breast-plate was ornamented with a harp surrounded with wreaths of shamrocks.

JOHN DWYER.

In the city of Philadelphia, died in exile, John Dwyer, an Invincible. He was buried on Sunday morning, October 7th, 1883, and Dan Boland, writing of the patriot's death to *United Ireland*, said : " Dwyer's remains were followed to the grave by a sorrowing crowd of sympathetic mourners, representing nearly every county at home, from Fair Head to Cove, and from Galway to Dublin. Another victim to Saxon rule, brave John Dwyer, at the age of twenty years, was laid to rest far from the dear, old land, ever and always the chief object of his love.

Sorrowful as was the occasion, not an exile present whose blood did not circulate more rapidly with joyful pride at sight of the pall-bearers, " Invincibles" also in heart and soul. I need ask no pardon for naming Pat Molloy, Mike Murphy, Tom Martin, and last, but not least, Pat Canton—four boys who, together with other " Invincibles" here, hope and pray for active service once more. At the grave, when the clods fell with hollow sound on the coffin of as brave and patriotic a boy as ever sought to " remove" a tyrant, I am sure not many present but mentally cursed the rule which consigned him to an early grave ; and if the truth was known, many a stern resolve was made ere quitting that newly-made turf mound to *practically* help her cause in future—poor, down-trodden, dear old Motherland.

Poor John Dwyer, taken from off his sick-bed in Dublin during the time of the late arrests there, and hurried to Kilmainham Prison, his constitution did not stand the confinement and rigorous discipline of that jail, and when " the prosecution" saw he was doomed, he was offered his liberty on condition of leaving Ireland and go spend his remaining days on earth in some other land. But, thank God, his last hours were brightened by the presence of old friends—exiled comrades from home.

God rest your soul, John Dwyer ! and may the foreign sod rest lightly on you, is the prayer of one who shall ever revere your memory, and the memory of the four noble souls whom you have already joined in the shadowy land—Eternity.''

" Invincibles'' we'll prove erelong, if we but do our part
And Dwyer's spirit animates each honest Irish heart ;
Yes ! please the Lord, who rules above, that day full soon shall come
When we'll avenge him and the boys who fought and died at home.

DAN. B.

Dwyer was arrested on a charge of conspiracy to murder. He was examined by the prison physicians, who pronounced him to be dying of consumption. He was released from Kilmainham Jail on March 31st, and a few months later came to Philadelphia.

JAMES MULLETT AND OTHERS.

JAMES MULLETT, Edward O'Brien, Edward McCaffrey, Daniel Delaney, William Moroney and Thomas Doyle, all of whom had pleaded guilty to the charge of conspiracy to murder, were arraigned in court for sentence May 17th, 1883.

The first five mentioned were each sentenced to ten years' penal servitude, and Doyle to five years' penal servitude. The Crown decided to drop the criminal charge against McCaffrey of having participated in the removal of Burke. Judge O'Brien, in passing sentence upon James Mullett, said : " There is no more known concerning you than has been made public. I believe you were present during the attack on Juror Field." Mullett replied, " I was not." The judge then adverted to the principal share the prisoner had taken in organizing the conspiracy to murder. Matthias Brady, who was charged with threatening the foreman of the jury which convicted his brother, Joe Brady, pleaded guilty to the charge, but the Crown and the person threatened assented to his discharge.

Peter Doyle, believed to be an Invincible, was also in court, but his trial was postponed on account of sickness. He was so weak that he had to be assisted to the dock by a warder.

JOSEPH POOLE.

Pistol shots were heard under the railway arch in Seville Place, Dublin, on the morning of July 4th, 1882, and persons that passed immediately before the firing overheard three men disputing. When the weapons were discharged two of the men ran away, and the third fell lifeless to the pavement. The body was recognized as that of John Kenny. On the remains was found a belt with the inscription " God save Ireland." The body had seven stabs and four bullet wounds. Kenny had been previously fired at. Joseph Poole and two others were arrested shortly after, and Poole was held for trial, while the other two were discharged. Subsequently several more arrests were made of parties suspected, but these men were also discharged. On September 19th, 1882, McCaffrey, Poole and Carey, who had been under arrest for the killing of Kenny, were released from custody. Poole was re-arrested on November 28th, on the occasion of the funeral of Detective Cox, and on the 29th was held for trial on a charge of being implicated in the shooting of Cox. On January 4th the trial of Poole was postponed until the next term of the Commission Court.

At the trial of Invincibles in Dublin, on January 27th, 1883, William Lamie, a brother-in-law of Poole, testified to Poole's being a member of the Vigilance Committee of Fenians which " removed" certain parties. On the 8th of February, P. Dowling was convicted of the " removal" of Detective Cox, and sentenced to penal servitude for life. This cleared Poole of that charge. On the 27th of April a printer named Gibney and Eugene Kingston were tried in Dublin on the charge of conspiracy to murder Poole, who was then a Fenian Centre, and who was alleged to have turned informer.

Perjured testimony was given at this trial by one Devine, an informer, that one Boland, a Fenian Centre, sentenced Poole to death and ordered Kingston to carry out the sentence. The society which condemned Poole to death also decided upon the " removals" of

Detective Cox, Judge Lawson, Director Jenkinson, of the Criminal Investigation Department, and Mallon, chief detective, and to blow up the house in which the government witnesses were lodging.

The same society, it was asserted, ordered the murders of Kenny and Bailey. He also testified that the same men who murdered Detective Cox were charged with the removal of Poole. On the 4th of May the above named were again examined, when William Lamie testified that Poole, his brother-in-law, came to him on the night of the removal of Kenny, and gave him a full account of how the deed was done. On the 11th of May Gibney and Kingston were held for trial, without bail, on the charge of conspiracy to murder Poole, and the Grand Jury, on May 16th, found true bills against them. Their trial was postponed until the next assizes. On June 8th both Kingston and Gibney were admitted to bail. On the same date the Court at Dublin acquitted Poole of the charge of conspiracy to murder, and he was immediately rearrested upon the charge of murdering Kenny.

From the start the Britishers had made up their minds to hang Poole, an innocent man, for the "removal" of Kenny, whom the Castle detectives said was a suspected traitor. They had no evidence save that of Lamie, and that they purchased. It was not, however, on evidence that the Castle hacks relied, but on a packed jury. After innumerable delays Poole's case came up on November 12th, 1883. The prisoner was defended by Dr. Webb and Mr. Moriarty. Porter, Attorney-General for Ireland, in opening the case for the prosecution, stated that it would not be proven that Poole inflicted the wounds that killed Kenny, but that he had lured Kenny to the place where the murder was committed, and that he was named by the Fenians as one of those delegated to commit the murder.

Dr. Webb opened the case for the defence. He said that he rose to discharge an onerous duty under somewhat unfavorable circumstances—to lay before them the case of the prisoner in opposition to what the Attorney-General, as he (Dr. Webb) submitted with great rhetorical exaggeration described as the overwhelming case against the prisoner presented by the Crown. He did not know that he was going beyond perhaps the privilege of an advocate when he said that he could not look upon his lordship, presiding with such dignity in

that court, without a flood of memories rushing back upon his mind
of the days when they were young together. He had watched his
career during the last quarter of a century ; he had watched his
brilliant career and recognized his brilliant leadership ; and he had
the pleasure of sympathizing with the feeling of every one regarding
his lordship's well-deserved promotion ; and he was sure that no judge
that ever sat upon the bench would do more ample justice to the prisoner, would more carefully sift the evidence, would more liberally
give him the benefit of every doubt and of every benefit which the law
conferred on him than would his lordship. It was in this spirit he (Dr.
Webb) approached the investigation of this most painful and most
anomalous, and most abnormal case. The position of Poole was somewhat peculiar. Openly and avowedly he was a member of what was
called the Fenian Brotherhood—a brotherhood which the Attorney-
General had observed had never done good to any human being.
But it was a brotherhood which had made history ; which had
roused statesmen from their slumbers ; which had brought measures
which seemed separated from them by immeasurable space within
measurable distance ; which had disestablished churches that seemed
based upon a rock ; unsettled settlements secured by conquest, by
legislation, and by time ; had modified the whole history of
Ireland, determined its legislation, and was at the present moment
exerting a powerful influence upon the annals of the empire. He
(Dr. Webb) said not this in praise. His sentiments were well
known. Every conviction of his mind, every sentiment of his heart,
every prejudice of his nature, was right against all the objects of this
organization. But he could not shut his eyes to facts, and these
facts had been irresistibly suggested to him by the very remarks
which the Attorney-General had made in his opening statement.
That organization was divided into two sections. The one to which
the prisoner belonged, which repudiated all anomalous, abnormal and
nefarious methods of carrying out its design, had no sympathy with
assassination ; dreamt not of employing the mysterious agencies of
nature to overwhelm in common ruin the innocent and those whom
they deemed to be guilty. His voice, like the voice of all those connected with the organization, was for war, but it was for honorable

war, " honorable" according to their conceptions of the case. In a moment of aberration Poole had been induced to leave the party with which he had hitherto been associated, and had joined the Council party—had joined the party that had adopted means and appliances which not only outraged public sentiments, but which outraged the milder and more constitutional party to which Poole himself had originally belonged. But he soon abandoned the Council party, and it was in evidence that he had fallen out with Daniel Curley, a man whose determined character and ruthless spirit was recorded in the page of history and in the annals of that very court. Poole had been regarded as a deserter, and had become the object of the deadly animosity of, and had been violently attacked by, Daniel Curley and a body of his men. At a subsequent period he was reported to the Vigilance Committee, the object of which was the removal of all obnoxious members. A conspiracy was formed for his death, and his death was considered of importance in order that he might no longer exert his influence to keep the Stephenite party together, and prevent its amalgamation with Curley's party. Now the " affair" in the Park, which occurred on the 6th of May, 1882, was perpetrated by parties, who, in the universal opinion, did not belong to the Stephenite party, but to the Council faction. On the 4th of July Kenny was " removed " under the railway arch in Seville Place ; on the 27th and 28th of November Cox, the constable, was killed in Abbey Street. On the 4th of July Poole was arrested, brought before a magistrate and committed, not on this charge, but as a suspect. He remained in prison until the 18th of September. He was arrested for the " removal " of Cox on the 28th of November—arrested for the " removal " of a man who was killed on the very night by the very persons who were on his (Poole's) own track, in order to " remove" him. He was kept in prison until the 8th of June, when he was discharged, but as he stepped forth from the Court he was again arrested for the present offence. During all that period Poole was in Kilmainham. They all knew the terrible tragedies that were enacted during the period within the Court and in the prison ; when informer after informer came forward, and when first Brady, then Curley, then Fagan, then Caffrey, then Timothy Kelly, died on the scaffold. During all that time Poole was in jail, and during all that time there was a busy devil whispering at his ear, " Save your life," " Inform," " Invent," " Secure the protection of the government," " Secure your life and affluence in some foreign clime ;" and during the whole of that time Poole maintained his ground and made no sign. The death bell of Joe Brady tolled in his ears and he was unmoved ; he heard the death-knell sound of Curley, and he was unshaken ; again he heard the doleful sound in the cases of Fagan, of Caffrey, and of Kelly, and he was mute. Now, he (Dr. Webb) cared not in what point of view they regarded this. Supposing that the Crown case was right, let them do justice to the man, even if they hanged him. A great poet told us there was somewhat still of good in things evil. Chivalry and heroism were not a monopoly of virtue. Indeed, it spoke well of the inherent dignity of human nature to find that even crime might be chivalrous and might be heroic ; and chivalry and heroism exhibited under such circumstances was the more wonderful and the more creditable because it was exhibited when divested of its great security, its protection, and its animating spirit —virtue and innocence. Now, this man who exhibited these high qualities was the man whom the Crown charged with being a party to a foul and unnatural murder. Whatever philosophers might say, and men who talked of their practical experience might prate, there was a consistency in human character, and he said it was incredible—that might be too strong a word—but it was unlikely to the last degree, that a man who had displayed such chivalry and such heroism, and such loyalty to his own party, should have been guilty of so base, so brutal, so foul, and so unnatural an " affair" as this. Counsel con- tended that the case made for the Crown, so far from being over- whelming and coercive, was singularly weak, and its weakness was only partly concealed by the cloud of witnesses with which they had enveloped and disguised it.

The judge charged against the prisoner. He said : The prisoner did not appear to have gone to Grenville Street next morning to take his breakfast.

The Prisoner.—I did not take my meals in Grenville Street at all. I ate at Lamie's place always.

The " Judge."—Quite right.

The Prisoner.—He is acting the part of a prosecutor in place of a judge.

The " Judge."—Quite right. He might have eaten in Lamie's place ; but there was not a particle of evidence to prove that he slept in his own house that night. That was the case made by the Crown and commented on by counsel for the defence. They relied upon the fact that in Kenny's house the evidence only showed that it was Kenny who consented to go out with Poole. But still he went with him, and further than the corner of the lane, and he went with him —he thought admittedly—to the arch, and there he was murdered. If they had a doubt, they were bound to give him the benefit of it. If not—if the evidence led them to the highest degree of moral certainty that could be attained by evidence, and satisfied them that the prisoner was privy to the assassination of Kenny on that night—privy to it in the sense that he knew beforehand that it was to be committed, was with him knowing it was to be committed—it did not matter whether he raised a hand to strike him at all—they were bound by the oaths they had taken, and by their duty to society and to their country, to bring in that verdict which the evidence demanded from their consciences.

There was, at least, one honest man in that jury-box who would not consent to do the bidding of the bloodthirsty British horde. He would not consent to sign the death-warrant of an innocent man against whom there was not a particle of honest testimony. The jury was thereupon discharged, and Poole was remanded to prison.

That the Britishers were determined to hang Poole was apparent when, on the 19th of the same month, he was again placed at the bar. A jury had in the mean time been " fixed," and evidence or no evidence they were prepared to render a verdict of " guilty" to please the hounds whose mean tools they were.

At the opening of the second trial of Poole his counsel, Dr. Webb, urged that the trial could not now proceed, as, the case being conducted under the Crimes Act, a formal notice should have been given to the accused, which had not been done. Justice Murphy held that the notice given to the accused upon the previous trial was

sufficient, but promised the defendant's counsel that he would make
a note of the objection thus raised.   A jury was thereupon em-
panelled.   The court room was crowded.

Porter, for the prosecution, recounted the evidence given at the
former trial, and submitted to the Court that it proved that Poole
was privy to the design of the Fenians to remove Kenny, and that if
he did not actually inflict the wounds upon Kenny he lured the victim to his doom and was present at the murder.

On the second day of the "judicial farce," William Lamie repeated his former evidence.

Dr. Webb, addressing the court, held that there was no evidence
whatsoever from which the jury could infer that Poole's was the
hand that fired the shot or struck the blow, depriving him of life.
There was no evidence that he aided in the commission of the crime,
and there was no evidence that he had acted in concert with others for
that purpose, and as these were the triple heads of the indictment,
the prisoner was, in strictness of law, entitled to a direction from his
lordship on all the points.

The "Justice" said he did not understand the point.   The indictment was a simple one for murder, and he could not tell the jury that
there was no evidence to support a capital charge.

Dr. Webb in his address to the jury mentioned that the jury were
selected from a class which was animated by a stern determination,
and very right, though a stern one, to suppress disorder and restore
law and order to the realm.   The one question here was, Had the
crime of murder been brought home to the prisoner with that plenitude of proof that their consciences demand, and that their oath must
extort ?   They were not there to save society—nor to crush nefarious
organizations ; but they were to decide the question, as if these were
the most peaceful times.   He had hitherto reviewed the case without
dealing with the evidence of Lamie.   If ever there was a monster in
human form that must have excited their loathing it was that man.
The inspired Word told them that the "Fear of the Lord is the beginning of wisdom," and there was no higher courage than the fear
of their own conscience ; no fear higher than the fear of doing harsh,
unjust, and wicked things ; and if they found a verdict against the

prisoner, who was now imploring them from British justice, when the British law gave him the benefit of a doubt, and if they did not give him it they robbed him of it not the less because he was a Fenian or a rebel, or because he disagreed with them, or was a member of an organization that had paralyzed commerce, and that had arrested enterprise in the development of the country. If there was a doubt upon their mind, if on the evidence they believed that the case was not clearly proved, let them say to the Crown authorities that they had not fulfilled the onus of proof cast upon them, that they had not produced that plenitude of proof that satisfied them (the jury), that they had not proved the case, and if they thought the case was not proven, then, in God's name, and in anticipation of His judgment, let them pronounce boldly and fearlessly the verdict of "Not Guilty." (Applause.)

The Attorney-General replied on the part of the Crown. In concluding his charge, the Judge said : " They were bound to be scrupulous in their examination of the evidence. To use the words of a judge and not an advocate, they were there to acquit him if they could, convict him if they must. They had nothing to fear, if they were firm and just. They should act, however, as faithful, honest citizens, anxious to discharge their duty toward their God and their country."

At twenty minutes to six o'clock the jury retired, and at a quarter past six o'clock came again into court with a verdict of guilty.

When asked in the usual formal manner by Clerk Geale, if he had anything to say why sentence of death should not be passed upon him, the prisoner, who stood forward, with one hand on the dock, said : " Well, gentlemen, you have found me guilty of the murder of John Kenny : I wish to say in the presence of this crowded court, in the presence of my fellow-countrymen that I love, that it is false. The man that says I was guilty of the murder of John Kenny is a liar. I have been a member of the Irish Republican Brotherhood, and I am proud to be a member, and I would be proud to go to the scaffold for being a member of the Irish Republican Brotherhood. Our objects were not for murder. Our objects were to free Ireland from the tyrannical rule it is under. They have brought forward my brother-in-law, Lamie, the man that tried to have me murdered, the man that tried to murder others—that is the evidence of another wretch of a man. My counsel has ably depicted him in language that I could not make use of. There are many points my counsel has not brought forward that I wished to have him bring forward. Of course he knows his own reason far better than I do. There is one thing that I would have wished him to have brought forward. That is regarding Superintendent Mallon asking another person for to swear false in this case ; and if they were guilty of asking one party to swear false they have not been backward in asking another. Shortly after my release from under the Coercion Act a young girl of the name of Lizzie Kearns, living in Marlborough Street, was brought down to the detective office by Mr. Eastwood and Mr. Stratford. Mr. Mallon told her he had received information that she was in Seville Place on the night of the murder, and saw the murder committed. The young girl denied it. After she denied it he asked her would she admit being there, if Francis Grundy, her sweetheart, was released from prison. She still refused. He then asked her if Francis Grundy sent her a message out of prison would she swear that she was there to get him out of prison, and he would place Grundy in a position to marry her. Gentlemen of the jury, when Mr. Mallon—when these Crown officials were guilty of that, and got to asking Lizzie Kearns to swear false, they have not been backward in asking Lamie. Gentlemen, I didn't deny, when being arrested on the 4th of July, being along with Kenny. I acknowledged going home with Kenny that evening and leaving the place with Kenny that night, so that when I acknowledged that on that occasion, I could not have asked Lamie to get other parties to swear I was elsewhere that night. My lords, I am not accountable if the man who was struck down by my side—which is false—I am not accountable for the death of the man, even though it was a member of my own party which did it. I have been a member of the Irish Republican Brotherhood since I was eighteen years of age, but never have I been connected with the Vigilance or any secret clubs which may be belonging to the organization. My object was simply to wait until such time as my countrymen would be prepared to strike a blow for independence, when I intended to take part with them. My object was not murder. I say again that it is false that I had anything to do with the killing of Kenny, or knew anything about it previous to his being murdered. If I had known about it I would not have went home with Kenny that night. I would have had it arranged, if I was the party to do it, that Kenny would have been deprived of his life on his way home. It is a mere nonsensical idea to say that if I had known it I would have walked home with the man and left his place with him. I again declare my innocence. I believe it is on account of being an enemy, humble as I am, of the government under which I have the misfortune to live that I have been persecuted in the manner I have been. Still I am not afraid to die, or ashamed of what has brought me to the scaffold. It is not for murder ; it is for being a member of the Irish Republican Brotherhood that has brought me to the scaffold, and I am prepared to die for it. There is one thing I would like to say to my fellow-countrymen and some people I see here (the prisoner then addressed the people in the gallery). I am thankful to you for having placed such implicit confidence in me, even knowing the temptation I am surrounded with. I am thankful to you, gentlemen, and if it is not out of place, farewell to all—farewell to Ireland. Three cheers for the Irish Republic, and to hell with English tyranny.''

The father, who was in the gallery, here began to weep loudly, and called out—'' O Joe—my Joe !''

Prisoner.—Father, keep—father, keep—

Mr. Poole was then helped out of court, sobbing loudly. In the street he was surrounded by a number of friends.

'' Justice'' Murphy then sentenced Poole to be hanged on December 18th

The prisoner, who did not seem to be much affected by the sentence, addressing the judge, said : '' My lord, one thing more. Allow me to thank (nodding to his counsel) my able counsel who so ably defended me. I am also thankful to the members of the Irish Republican Brotherhood who have so kindly subscribed to my defence.''

Poole was then removed.

The following composed the special jury that did the Britishers' dirty work : Adam Phayre, 6 Hume Street, lodging-house keeper (foreman) ; Luke Toole, D'Olier Street, seed merchant ; John Beatty, Grafton Street, carpet manufacturer ; Robert Geoghegan Trimbleston, Booterstown, civil engineer ; Archibald Wardlaw, D'Olier Street, gentleman ; John Findlater, Upper Sackville Street, wine merchant ; William Macklin, Crofton Terrace, Kingstown, plumber ; David Robert Little, Woodpark, Monkstown, gentleman ; Robert Richardson, Monkstown Lodge, Monkstown, grocer ; William R. Jones, Tudor Hall, Monkstown, barrister ; George O'Neill, Henry Street, magistrate ; Charles J. Evans, Upper Georges Street, Kingstown, shopkeeper.

Irishmen will remember them.

A few days after the conviction of Poole, Dr. Webb renewed his application for a writ of *certiorari* to bring into court the record in the case of the Queen *v.* Joseph Poole, tried at the last commission for the murder of John Kenny, in order that the verdict therein might be set aside, that the judgment therein might be vacated, and that a *venire de novo* might be directed on the ground that the alleged trial was a mistrial, inasmuch as it was had before a jury not competent to try the case. There was considerable discussion for and against the motion, at end of which " Justice" Lawson announced the decision of the court to be, no rule on the motion. That was the last appeal.

After his conviction Joseph Poole was removed from Kilmainham Jail to Richmond Prison. While awaiting execution he was visited three times a day by the Rev. W. S. Donegan, of Harolds Cross. Poole maintained his spirits throughout, and save on the final visit of his relatives he never gave way to any display of grief—much less of despondency. He slept well during his last night on earth, and rose shortly before six o'clock on the morning of his last day, December 18th, 1883. The chaplain arrived soon after. The time was spent in prayer until a quarter past seven o'clock, when Poole, accompanied by Father Donegan and the Rev. Canon Fricker, who had arrived in the interval, was conducted to the chapel. Mass was celebrated, and the Viaticum was administered to Poole, who had received Holy Communion on the previous day.

While the prison bell was tolling Poole with firm step walked between the Rev. Canon Fricker and Father Donegan to the gallows. They were followed by an acolyte carrying a crucifix. After them came a batch of warders. On the procession emerging from the pinioning-room the door leading to the scaffold was thrown open, and Poole, followed by the two clergymen, by the executioner, and two or three of the warders, walked firmly up the half dozen steps leading to the platform. The structure was an entirely new one. The platform, which forms also a covering for the pit underneath, was of wood, and raised three feet above the level of the yard, the drop having been obtained by excavating to the depth of about eight feet, the total height from the bottom of the pit to the roof being a little over eleven feet. The cross-beam to which the rope was fastened was of iron ; it stretched across the entire width of the yard, and fixed in the walls on either side, already mentioned. The rope was fastened to this beam, and four or five coils were rolled round it, the somewhat sharp edges of the iron bar conveying to the spectator the impression that the effect of a sudden jerk might be to cut the rope and cause it to give way. It was also noticeable that the last coil of the rope was fastened to the one next to it by a piece of ordinary whipcord. The entire structure was evidently intended to be permanent.

Poole took his place under the drop with the utmost fortitude, never for a moment ceasing to utter the responses to the prayers. The executioner proceeded to adjust the rope, which he did without delay. All preparations having been completed, the executioner stepped to the lever, and moved it, and the trap doors gave way, and Joseph Poole was no longer visible save to those alongside the drop and to Dr. Minchin, who, watch in hand, stood at the lower entrance to the pit, to time the period that elapsed between the drop and the extinction of life. Dr. Minchin stated that life was extinct in three and a half seconds, and in the evidence given by him subsequently at the inquest he said that death was instantaneous. As soon as the black wooden coffin was closed, a procession was formed, and headed by Father Donegan, with the cross bearer and acolytes, proceeded to the place of interment. This is a small quadrangular yard adjacent to the hospital. A newly opened grave, lying immediately beside Carr's, was waiting to receive the remains. The coffin was borne on the shoulders of four warders, and lowered by them. As soon as Father Donegan blessed the grave (which was quickly filled up), the recitation of the "De Profundis" closed the end of the sorrowful chapter. Immediately after the execution Father Donegan arrived in the hospital for the purpose of consoling the afflicted father, sister, and sister-in-law of the patriot.

The executioner, whose real name is said to be William Jones, is a native of Wales.

PATRICK O'DONNELL.

BECAUSE he was Irish born and a naturalized citizen of the United States, and had in self-defence shot down one of the vilest wretches that ever drew breath, the English Government were satisfied that Patrick O'Donnell was an Invincible, and therefore, after packing a jury and going through the farce of a trial, hanged him. O'Donnell's life was offered up as a sacrifice, and around the grave of the martyred dead Irishmen have united and sworn vengeance. It was not an idle oath they took, but one solemn and sincere. They will choose their own time, but the hanging of O'Donnell will not be forgotten. America begged a respite for the patriot, but it was refused. To Irishmen it was well that it was, for it kindled the spark into an unquenchable flame which to-day bids fair to destroy the British Empire.

Patrick O'Donnell, aged forty-eight years, a puddler of Gwedore, Donegal, had certainly a strange and eventful history. Illiterate, ordinarily inoffensive, a soldier in the American Civil War, thrifty, so that he became an investor in the Pennsylvania silver mines ; deprived by misfortune of the fruits of his thrift, the owner of a public-house in Canada, and again the possessor of a small fortune ; an investor of Fenian bonds, and once more left poor by commercial failure ; a returning emigrant to his native country ; then over to Scotland and the inmate of a hospital in Edinburgh ; from thence a roamer a second time to the American continent, for which he had taken the oath of citizenship in 1879, and a restless traveller back to Ireland in the beginning of June, 1883. These are the heads of the first half of his career. The second half opens as he leaves Donegal at the close of the same month for South Africa. Upon the same day a woman with seven children—three boys and four girls—take steerage passage for Natal in the same vessel under the name of Power. She was in reality Mrs. Carey, and the children include that extraordinary youth, Thomas Francis Carey, of whom Denman said that he was

" very clever and, indeed, over-astute." At Dartmouth, on the Dorset coast, James " Power" was put on board by his Irish detective companions on July 6th, possessed of a revolver, which he was given five days previous by Mr. Superintendent Mallon, and a check for £100 upon a bank at Natal, which had come from the Crown. At Madeira " Power" went ashore, and after the Kinfauns Castle left that island there was no further stoppage before Cape Town. O'Donnell had a revolver also—an electro-plated weapon of five chambers, and he amused himself shooting flying fish. Early on the morning of Friday, July 27th, the steamer entered Cape Town harbor, and the entire party, O'Donnells and " Powers," landed. O'Donnell and his associate, James " Power," sought the theatre, but finding it closed, went to a drinking shop together, and did not return to the Kinfauns Castle until eight or nine o'clock at night. Next day (Saturday) the passengers for Port Natal and other places on the south and east coasts of Cape Colony were transferred to the Melrose. O'Donnell had been prevailed upon by his unknown friend to continue his voyage to Natal, as being a better district for work than Cape Town, and the Melrose left for that port between five and six o'clock on Saturday evening. But in the course of that day, unfortunately for O'Donnell, it began to be whispered about that his boon companion, the so-called " Power," was none other than the informer Carey. A portrait was shown at Cape Town by a fellow-passenger to O'Donnell, purporting to be the likeness of Carey, and in the features O'Donnell sees the man who had been passing under the *nom de plume* " James Power." He puts the portrait in his pocket and goes on board. The Melrose has touched at and passed Algoa Bay, and is not far from Port Elizabeth, when O'Donnell, on the settee in the second saloon or general cabin, was drinking ale with Carey, who was standing in a lounging attitude against the side of the cabin. Carey was drinking O'Donnell's health, who had " stood the ale," and they clink their glasses ; the boatswain was playing at the cabin door with one of Carey's daughters ; Mrs. Carey is in her berth ; Carey himself was casually noticed conversing as if he were " laying down the law," beating his hand for emphasis as he spoke to O'Donnell. [Was Carey justifying the hanging of the Phœnix Park

men ?] And then, suddenly, a shot. Carey staggers back, hit on
the right side of the neck by a bullet which goes round his throat,
and passes out at the back. As he turns to rush to his wife's cabin,
O'Donnell fires a second shot, which takes effect in Carey's shoulder.
Mrs. Carey rushes from her berth, and Carey falls into her arms ex-
claiming, "O Maggie, I am shot!" and then O'Donnell dis-
charges a third chamber of his revolver, which lodges in the small of
Carey's back. This last, according to the doctor's evidence, was the
mortal wound. O'Donnell replaces his revolver in his pocket, but
surrendered to the boatswain. Just about the same moment occurred that alleged conversation between Mrs. Carey and O'Donnell,
which caused so much contradiction at the trial, and concerning
which Denman suggested to the jury whether they " ought not to
drop it altogether from their consideration." Carey when he was
shot was laid upon the cabin table ; a surgeon happening to be on
board attended him ; but, without speaking a word, he passed into
eternity in half an hour. O'Donnell was brought to Natal, examined before the magistrates there, committed to England, from
which he sailed on August 28th in the Athenian, and having entered
Plymouth Sound at noon on September 17th and dropped anchor off
Portland next morning to wait for daylight, he was ultimately landed
at Southampton on September 18th and conveyed to London. Then
came two examinations at Bow Street on that day and the 25th,
when he was fully committed, and his two days' trial at the Old
Bailey before "Justice" Denman.

Intense interest was shown by the public when O'Donnell came up
for trial. All the approaches to the court were thronged long before the hour appointed for the beginning of the proceedings. In
consequence of this, extraordinary difficulty was experienced, even
on the part of those having business there, in gaining admittance.

The prisoner, for whom a plea of not guilty was entered, seemed
perfectly composed as he was ushered into and stood up in the dock.
He had a sharply intelligent countenance, clean shaven, except for his
short whiskers, and was tall and well formed, though slim in body.
He glanced curiously about the court from time to time, and seemed
as if he were indulging in the habit of chewing, though whether he

had been favored with a supply of tobacco or was rolling about in his mouth an imaginary quid was a problem to the onlookers.

The Attorney-General and Mr. Poland appeared for the prosecution. Mr. C. Russell and Mr. A. M. Sullivan for the defence.

A jury having been sworn against all the rules of law, the Attorney-General opened the case for the Crown.

Thomas Francis Carey examined by the Attorney-General.—I was fifteen years of age last April. Up to July last I had lived in Dublin. My father had been in prison some time. On July the 4th I went on board the Kinfauns Castle with my mother and six brothers and sisters. We all went by the name of Power, except one who was called M'Kenna.

Did you notice what O'Donnell and your father were doing? No, they were speaking together. I did not hear any high words or anything to attract attention until the shot was fired.

Tell us what you saw? I saw Mr. O'Donnell draw a revolver from his pocket.

What did he do with it? He fired at my father, and the bullet hit him in the neck. My father was standing and the prisoner was sitting.

When the bullet hit your father, what did he say or do? I don't think he spoke, but I saw him stagger toward my mother's cabin.

What did you do? I ran toward my mother's cabin.

What for? To get my father's revolver.

When you got back into the saloon, where was your father, and in what position? My father was running toward my mother, and the prisoner fired the second shot. My father cried out, "O Maggie, Maggie, I am shot!" When the third shot was fired my father was standing with his face toward my mother. He had his back toward O'Donnell. I kept the pistol in my pocket.

Margaret Carey testified.—On the way out we made the acquaintance of the prisoner. He and my husband were on friendly terms together at Cape Town. We did not sleep on shore, but were transferred from one vessel to the other. On the afternoon of the following Sunday the prisoner and my husband were drinking ale together when I left them.

What first attracted your attention ? I heard a shot fired, but I thought it was a beer-bottle. When I heard a second I put the baby down and ran out. My husband ran to me and fell into my arms, saying, " O Maggie, I'm shot ! O'Donnell has shot me." He was bleeding.

Had you seen your son ? He ran into the cabin as I was coming out. I then heard the third shot. My husband and I fell together on the deck.

State all you remember. I said, " O'Donnell, this is my husband," and he said, " Shake hands, Mrs. Carey ; don't blame me, I was sent to do it." Up to that we had always passed by the name of Power. I knew my husband had a revolver, but I had never seen it.

Robert Cubitt examined.—I live at North Walsham, Norfolk, and assist my father as ironmonger. My brother Frank and myself were passengers on board the Kinfauns Castle, and saw the prisoner and James Power. I did not know that the latter was Carey. They were on friendly terms. Our destination was the Cape, and my brother and I went ashore.

Did you see O'Donnell there ? Yes. I spoke to him.

What did you say ? I asked him if he had seen the portrait of Carey.

Did you produce it ? Yes.

What did he say ? He said, " I will shoot him." He asked me for the portrait, and I gave it to him. He went on board, and the ship sailed about a quarter of an hour afterward.

Did O'Donnell say, " I'll shoot him," with an air of bravado ? He was smoking at the time.

In fact, until you heard of Carey's death you did not attach any moment to the words ? I did not.

Mr. Beecher, second officer, and Captain Rhodes of the Melrose, were examined.

Chief Superintendent Mallon, of the Dublin force, said he handed the revolver produced to Carey on the 1st of July, having obtained it from Mr. Weekes.

Cross-examined—He knew Carey very well, and was frequently

present at the trials in Dublin. Carey was a strong man, but not particularly big.

Mr. Russell.—Was it in consequence of his share in murderous plots that the government refused to give him a free pardon?

Witness could not say what the government did. He did not receive a free pardon. Did not hear Carey abuse the government. His own admissions and witness's dealings with him led him to the conclusion that he was a thoroughly desperate man as regarded human life. He swore in men, some of whom were his equal, and he admitted his intention of getting the knives by which the murders were perpetrated sent as exhibits to the Dublin Exhibition.

Re-examined.—In all his attempts he took particular care of his own life, and but for the evidence he gave he would have been probably condemned. This evidence made him execrated by the Irish people, and special means had to be taken for his protection.

When the trial was resumed, Mr. Russell recalled the witness Beecher for further cross-examination. He said : When I went down into the saloon, upon hearing the pistol, it was rather dark, and I felt it more as I went down suddenly out of the daylight.

The case for the defence was then opened

Walter Young, examined by Mr. Sullivan.—I am a cab proprietor at Port Elizabeth, where I was born. I often drove Mrs. Carey and her son Thomas Francis.

Did you have any conversation with him? Yes ; one day he came up to me. I said to him, "You are a fine fellow. Why didn't you shoot O'Donnell when he shot your father?" He answered, "I hadn't the revolver. I went to get it in the cabin, and when I got there it was gone, because my father had it." I said, "It's a bad job. It is quite likely you will have to go to England, and if you had shot him there might have been no more about it."

Re-examined.—I am thirty-two years of age, and was born at Gampal River, in South Africa.

My friend has suggested you were of Irish parents? No ; we belong to the Church of England. (Laughter.)

Mr. Russell addressed the jury for the defence. He said that a grave responsibility rested upon him—viz. that of presenting to the jury, as clearly as he could, the case on the part of the prisoner. It was no affectation to say that he would have been extremely glad if the responsibility had rested upon some one else who was more experienced in cases in that court. He did not pretend to be without experience, but his experience was not great in cases of that kind. He thought he would not be appealing to the jury in vain, and he asked them to listen with special attention to all that he had to say. The prisoner was charged with the gravest crime known to the law— that of having wilfully, maliciously, and of malice aforethought killed and murdered James Carey. The prisoner admitted that he had killed Carey, but he denied that he had committed murder. The law presumed, justly and rightly, every man to be innocent until his guilt had been proved, and until the verdict of the jury had been passed upon the issue then being tried, no man was entitled to say that the prisoner was guilty of the charge which he had denied. There was one appeal he must here make, and that was, that the jury would not allow their minds to be in any way biassed by impressions which they might have formed out of court upon information which might have reached them through newspapers or from other sources. This was no formal appeal, because, if ever there was a case in which it was necessary that the jury should discard all else they had heard beyond that which had transpired in the court, it was this. Theories and suggestions had been put forward which, if not discarded, would be fatal to the prisoner. That Patrick O'Donnell shot James Carey was beyond question, but the question for consideration was whether it was murder or whether the act was committed in self-defence, in the sense that the shot was fired in view of reasonable apprehension of then present danger to life and limb on the part of O'Donnell. Then, again, if they thought there was not such danger, they would have to consider whether there was not such serious apprehension on the part of the prisoner as to justify the use of the pistol ; and, further, the question might arise whether the act was done in cold blood, or whether it was done in the conviction that he was himself in danger. The first of those points went with the question of self-defence, and if it could be established that it was in self-defence it would be their duty to say that the prisoner was not guilty. But if they came to the conclusion that there was reasonable apprehension, but not sufficient to justify the act, although they might not be inclined to let the man go free, they might think they were not justified in sacrificing his life to the law. Those were questions to which he would invite attention.

The Judge at this point interrupted the learned counsel, and said that he had a letter from a gentleman named Ayres, in Leadenhall Street, inclosing a letter to a juryman, in which it was stated that his wife was better.

A Juryman.—Thank you, my Lord ; she was dangerously ill.

The Judge.—I think it better I should keep the letter, but I have told you the contents.

Mr. Russell, resuming, said that he was pleased that the juryman, with sufficient anxiety of this case, should be spared serious domestic trouble. He was about to state some matters on which there was little difference of opinion. He agreed that, *prima facie*, every act of man-killing was murder ; but the same law that declared that, also declared that even if there was not a single fact or particle of direct evidence of acts of violence amounting to provocation or justification, it was still for the jury to decide whether there was a fair inference of such provocation or justification. For instance, if no one were present at the killing, it would still be for the jury to take all the surrounding circumstances into consideration, and decide whether there was not inference of provocation or justification, which would reduce the offence to manslaughter. He had said he made no formal appeal in asking them to discard all matters of prejudice, and he earnestly insisted on that appeal as if the facts and circumstances warranted them, and he hoped to satisfy them they did ; he wanted to get their minds wholly free from the idea that O'Donnell had the most remote conception when he went on board the Kinfauns Castle on the 4th of July, that either Carey or his family were going to be passengers on it. This the learned Attorney-General had laid down in his opening, but he wished, if possible, to make it clearer still, because he knew the insidious effect which statements out of doors might have upon them. It had been stated in the public press, and nothing could be more reprehensible, that O'Donnell had gone on board the Kinfauns Castle as an emissary, tracing Carey like a sleuthhound, and he wanted to show and demonstrate the utter groundlessness and falsity of such a suggestion. They knew the resources of the Crown, legal and detective, and it would be the duty of the Crown, which they would fail in, if having any evidence of premeditation on the part of Patrick O'Donnell, they did not bring it forward. No one could doubt they had discharged their duty, and he was justified in asking the jury to believe that the Crown, with their great detective power, had followed the career of Patrick O'Donnell through the wilds of Donegal and in America, to expose from beginning to end the life and incidents of the life of the prisoner down to the moment of his taking his passage to South Africa. They would have explained, if they could have done, the statement irresponsibly put forward that he knew Carey was to be a passenger on the Kinfauns Castle. He put this forward because the Crown had finally come to the conclusion that O'Donnell never knew until he got to the Cape that his fellow-passenger was James Carey. Why was it, how came it, that irresponsible writers and purveyors of news came to give this statement—

The Judge.—This is going a little too far, and is not, I think, in the interests of the prisoner. Surely the jury may be trusted not to believe anything except what is before them. You are commenting on something that is not in evidence.

Mr. Russell argued that it was decided in the Queen *v.* Barrett, in 1868, that contemporary matters could be brought forward by counsel. The Attorney-General of that day referred to the Fenian rising.

The Judge.—That was something like a matter of history, but this raises a difficult question, as you are referring to things I have never seen, having steadily refrained from reading anything about it. You are commenting on what probably not one of the jury has ever seen, and it is wide of the mark, especially after the full admission of the Attorney-General that up to the time of the arrival at the Cape it must be assumed, in favor of the prisoner, that he knew nothing of Carey.

Mr. Russell, resuming, said he would be content with that. Not to argue any further on the statements put forward, he would ask whether it would not enter naturally into the minds of persons, judging

from what happened, that on July 29th, when, without any apparent
provocation or even show of violence, this bloody deed should have
been done, one's mind naturally at once concluded that it was premeditated.   They recollected the language attributed by Mrs. Carey
to O'Donnell.   At Port Elizabeth, in Bow Street, and here, she attributed to the prisoner the words, "I was sent to do it." Her statement was unsupported by the other Crown witnesses, except so far as
it might be said to be supported by her son, Thomas Francis Carey.
They must view the boy's evidence with suspicion and distrust.   At
Port Elizabeth he said nothing about "I was sent to do it;" but at
Bow Street, having read his mother's evidence, he corroborated for
the first time the words he had read in his mother's evidence.   In the
cross-examination by his learned friend, Mr. Sullivan, at Bow Street,
he again and again reiterated the statement, until, on being pressed,
he was finally obliged to alter the language he had originally used.
He (the learned counsel) agreed it was enough to accept the Attorney-
General's statement.   They must take the basis that Patrick
O'Donnell, a man whose hands bore the marks of hard but honest
labor, was going peacefully in the Kinfauns Castle, harboring no
thought of James Carey.   Until he arrived at the Cape he was ignorant of his presence, and James Carey did not think he was identified.
O'Donnell was one actor, and the other was Carey.   He agreed that
the vilest character was entitled to the protection of the law, and
that even James Carey was entitled to that protection.   It was no
less a murder, if it was a murder, because the man was James Carey.
But it was necessary they should see who James Carey was, because
it would be impossible to realize, as he hoped to make them realize,
the position of things when the two men found themselves face to
face on July 29th, unless they had an adequate conception of what
the other man was.   He would not disturb the slumbering ashes of
the dead, but it could not be dispensed with, and he should present
them with something of the portraiture of James Carey.   He did not
want to enlarge on his wickedness, but would call attention to him
when he found that not only O'Donnell but all the people on board
knew him, and to which he had called the attention of his son on
leaving Cape Town.   He called attention to this because he proposed

to show that James Carey was a cruel and treacherous man, who, finding a man who had detected him, would not hesitate to make a show of violence at least, even if he did not actually put it in force. Inspector Mallon had said in the box that James Carey through all his acts had taken care to protect his own skin, and when he found himself face to face with one of his own countrymen who had named him he would not have hesitated, coward as he was, to shoot the man, particularly as he would have known under the circumstance that he could do so with practical impunity. He wanted to make out that as soon as the mask was torn from his face that Carey became a desperate man. That the man was utterly regardless of human life was shown by the part he took in the Phœnix Park murders. Unhappily grave crimes had stained the soil of Ireland, but none so grave as that; but no one dreamt that James Carey, the Dublin builder, the Christian man, the member of secret societies, was one of the actors in that awful tragedy. Carey was afterward arrested, with others, but was taken from the dock to give evidence for the Crown. He could imagine a case of a man who became penitent after committing a great crime and gave evidence, but that was not the case with Carey, who only became an informer to save his own neck. From first to last he did not show a particle of regret for what he had done ; on the contrary, he seemed to glory in it, and refused to call it murder, saying it was that simply " removal." In the Park itself he went to point out his victim. That man had to flee the country, execrated by all, for a viler thing never assumed human form. He left the country unpardoned by his Queen and unforgiven by his God, his hand against every man and every man's conscience against him. Such a man would not hesitate to use a deadly weapon upon provocation, however slight. It might be said that all this went to show that it would be more likely that a man like O'Donnell should have taken Carey's life. He wished to meet that fairly and fully. He agreed that it would be so, but the jury must bring their own common-sense to bear, and ask themselves whether a man with deadly intentions would not, in the selection of time and place, have shown some desire to shield himself from the consequences of his act. Did it appear likely that without any previous quarrel or disturbance,

O'Donnell would, under such circumstances, have selected a time when there were seven persons present, when he was within forty-eight hours of Natal, and within reasonable distance of the security and secrecy of the bush ? Let them bear that in their minds. He did not think his learned friend in his high judicial position, desiring only the vindication of the law, would condescend to argue the case with the tenacity of a struggle at nisi prius. The Attorney-General, he trusted, would remember he was a minister of the law, and he (the learned counsel) trusted, would ask for their consideration of the case without any heat of advocacy to divert their judgment from the fair issue of the case. The vessel arrived at the Cape early in the morning of Friday, July 27th, and up to that moment no one dreamed that Power was James Carey. On that day the passengers went on shore, and on the Saturday some of them left the vessel and again went up town. James Carey admittedly did so on Friday, accompanied by Patrick O'Donnell, and, finding the theatre closed, they went to a drinking saloon. On Saturday they were transferred to the Melrose Castle early in the day, and it sailed from the Cape about five o'clock on Saturday evening. Did James Carey go ashore on the Saturday afternoon ? His son Thomas said he did not, but Mrs. Carey said he did, and that he was accompanied by Thomas Carey. They therefore had it that up to that time there was not only no ill-will between Carey and O'Donnell, but they had the significant facts that during the voyage out they had got to be friends or chums ; that Carey pointed out there was more chance of employment at Natal, and that finally O'Donnell agreed to go on there, and was transferred to the Melrose, with James Carey and his family. The law was that the prisoner could not come into the witness-box and testify either on or without oath as to the facts, though he (the learned counsel) hoped to see the day when such a thing was permitted, as he believed it would further the ends of justice. Some judges had allowed the prisoner, notwithstanding being represented by counsel, to make a statement, but commonly and ordinarily the prisoner's mouth was closed. He therefore proposed briefly to tell the story of this occurrence as told by the man himself. Mrs. Carey mentioned a circumstance not adverted to by any one else, that there was some conversation about O'Donnell's pistol at the Cape on board the Melrose, and that O'Donnell stated he had sold the pistol. The statement made to him (Mr. Russell) by the prisoner was that that conversation was true, and that it occurred between James Carey and the prisoner at the bar. Did not that fit in actually with some of the facts deposed to by the Crown witnesses? The condition of things then was that James Carey knew he was recognized. What was the first thing that would occur to his mind? He would know that he was an object of dislike to all honest minds, and especially to a man like O'Donnell. The first thing which would occur to him would be, " Is there danger about?" Mrs. Carey had shown that there was an apprehension of possible danger by her statement that Carey asked O'Donnell when on the ship whether he still had his pistol. When asked, he said he had disposed of it at Cape Town. Therefore the condition of things was this, that Carey thought O'Donnell had not his pistol. The theory of the Crown was that Patrick O'Donnell, when he had abundant opportunities of making away with the man he hated, with security to himself, selected Sunday, the 29th of July, at 3.45 in the afternoon, when there were several other persons present. This was not all, for they said that the act was done in this way. O'Donnell sitting down, Carey standing up, and no quarrel, the man is described as having without any excitement killed his man. This is what they stated; but what was the true position of affairs? It was admitted that the boatswain, O'Donnell, Carey, and Mrs. Carey were present, but it was strongly denied that Parish was present when the first shot was fired. The case for the prisoner, as he stated the facts, showed that there was substantial truth in the evidence of Jones, Beecher, and Marks, but he asked the jury to discredit that of Mrs. Carey and the son. Referring to the relations which existed between Carey and O'Donnell on board the ship, the learned counsel said that when O'Donnell discovered that Power was Carey he did not want to have anything further to do with him, upon which Carey asked him why, and O'Donnell tried to evade the question.

The Attorney-General desired to take his Lordship's opinion as to the admissibility of the statement which was made by the prisoner to a third party. These statements were spoken of as facts, and it was really making the counsel in the case a witness.

The Judge.—Do I understand that you wish to state that which was told by the prisoner to another person ?

Mr. Russell.—Yes.

The Judge.—Then I hold that it is not admissible.

Mr. Russell said that he simply sought to do that which was allowed in the case of the Queen *v.* Weston. He proposed to give the jury the prisoner's own statement as to the matter.

The Judge.—I do not think I can admit it.

Mr. Russell said he proposed to tell the jury that it was not proved in evidence, but it was the prisoner's account of the matter, and it was for the jury to judge, in view of the proven evidence in the case, how far it was consistent with the evidence. In other words, it was what the prisoner would have a right to say if he was not represented by counsel.

The Judge.—The point is important, and there is much difference of opinion on it.

Mr. Russell called attention to the Queen *v.* Weston, where two men were in a house alone, and one was shot dead. Mr. Kingsford, who represented the prisoner, said he could not give his version of the matter ; but the Lord Chief Justice of England—before whom the case was being heard—ruled that he could do so. What he proposed to do was to give the prisoner's own account, for the jury either to disregard or reject if they thought proper.

The Judge said there was a great preponderance in judicial opinion against the admission of such a statement. If an objection was taken, it might be necessary for him to reserve a case upon it.

The Attorney-General.—I have no objection to my learned friend stating the defence.

The Judge asked if there was any practical worth in the objection. Mr. Russell was entitled to say this or that was supposed to have taken place, and to ask the jury whether all the circumstances did not point to it being so.

The Attorney-General thought it would be most objectionable and most unsatisfactory in a criminal case to have any question reserved, and therefore he withdrew his objection.

Mr. Russell, continuing, said that counsel had been allowed to state hypothetical cases, and then ask the jury whether they were not likely to be absolute facts. He was, however, stating to the jury what the prisoner's own statement was, exactly as the prisoner would be entitled to state it himself if unrepresented by counsel. No effect could, however, be given to that statement except, and it was an important exception, that it fitted in with the evidence of the Crown. If, however, it filled in the blanks and afforded the true clew to the awful occurrence, then, and then only, they would give effect to it. To resume, O'Donnell and Carey were seated side by side in apparent friendliness. O'Donnell told him he would have nothing more to do with him. On being pressed by Carey, O'Donnell said, "I want to have nothing to do with an informer." Carey said, "What do you mean by an informer?" O'Donnell then turned round and said, "You are James Carey, the damned Irish informer." On this Carey sprang to his feet and produced a weapon, but O'Donnell was quicker in pulling his out, and shot at Carey. That was the prisoner's account of the matter, and they must see how it fitted the account given by the Crown witnesses. First of all, there was not a syllable of that inconsistent with the evidence of those called for the Crown, except James Parish and Francis Carey. Except those two, no one suggested they saw the first shot fired. It would be asked why there was no altercation and high words. The scene he had attempted to describe was a short one. James Carey found himself face to face with O'Donnell, countryman of his own, to protect and guard himself against whom the Government had given him a weapon of defence. He found himself in the presence of a man who said he wanted to have nothing to do with him, and called him James Carey, the damned Irish informer." What would be the most likely thing for a coward like Carey to do, armed as he was with a weapon that the Government had furnished him with? Of course it would be to produce it, either for the purpose of a deadly use to give effect to show of violence. If that were the true statement of the case, the prisoner's life ought not to be forfeited to the law. How did that fit the evidence? He had asked them not to rely upon the evidence of James Parish and Thomas Carey; if this were the true account it was said to be, was not attention drawn to the cabin? But his answer was that such a scene would only occupy the briefest moment. Parish had said that which was not reliable, even if he did not intentionally mistate. He had said that he saw the first shot fired, which was untrue. Thomas Francis Carey, in cross-examination, said that his father must have seen Jones, but not Parish, who came out of the cabin after the first shot was fired, and that substantially accorded with what Parish himself was forced to admit when he was cross-examined. That young Carey did not lack acuteness and intelligence of a high order was evident, and he had not been brought up in a good school for truth. Under these circumstances, could he be accepted as a reliable witness? He hoped to show by his own account that he could not. He said that he was at the end of the cabin, nearest the companion steps. Jones was playing with the little sister, and he (young Carey) was looking at them. If that were so, he could not have seen the first shot fired, as described. If the evidence of those two witnesses was not reliable, what other evidence existed which conflicted with the prisoner's own account? He ventured to say none. Upon the evidence of Thomas Francis Carey the younger, they ought not to sacrifice the life of the humblest creature which existed. He told a circumstantial story of a conversation with his mother about the pistol, but the mother denied that such a conversation had ever taken place, or that she had seen the pistol as stated. Again, he said that when the ship arrived at Cape Town his father did not go on shore, but Mrs. Carey said that the father and son went on shore together. Next he said he took the bag from the Kinfauns Castle to the Melrose Castle, but Mrs. Carey had sworn that she took the bag. Thus in three particulars the boy had been proved by the evidence of his own manner to have been lying. Then the story with which he supported his assertion that his father did not take his pistol on shore was as unreliable as any of the others. He would ask them to believe that the whole tale of the duty on firearms at the Cape was the invention of Thomas Carey. Turning to other matters, the theory originally propounded was that Mrs. Carey stated that O'Donnell said, "I was sent to do it." Young Carey gave a different statement, but having read his mother's evidence, he at Bow Street for the first time used the words, until he was shaken in cross-examination. Were all the facts indicative of honest evidence ? Would they in any case rely implicitly on the evidence of that young man ? With all deference to their independent judgment, he said they could not. If they discarded, or thought unreliable the evidence of young Carey and Parish as to seeing the first shot, there was nothing. inconsistent in the statement of the prisoner. The boatswain Jones had given his evidence honestly, though he might be mistaken in describing O'Donnell as sitting all through the three shots. That Carey was standing and O'Donnell sitting at the first shot was probable. Mr. Ensor, the surgeon, had said that the first shot might have been given in that position. If it were true that at the final moment, when Carey, alarmed, produced his weapon, Carey at the same time leaning over O'Donnell, then the direction of the wound might be where it was. As regarded the other two wounds, he thought Jones must have been mistaken, because under no conceivable circumstances could the wounds have been downward if the prisoner had remained sitting. Commenting on the evidence of Beecher and Marks, the learned counsel asked the jury to consider them as truthful witnesses. They had described the shots as having a pause after the first, and then two shots following in quick succession. If the jury were left at the end of their anxious consideration of the case with the belief that circumstances did exist which might have justified O'Donnell in firing the first shot, which would reduce the crime to manslaughter, then it required no argument to show that he could not be found guilty of murder by reason of the other shots in quick succession. In other words, if such a state of things existed as would justify him in self-defence firing the first shot by reason of his apprehension of violence, such provocation would reduce the offence to manslaughter, and nothing could be made of the second and third shots, which were virtually part of the same act, following one another in quick succession. The first observation he had to make about Cubitt's evidence was that on the part of the prisoner he was grateful to the Crown for calling him. But for that evidence O'Donnell might have been placed in a position of even greater danger by the possession of the portrait of Carey, which might have been regarded as a strong evidence of premeditation. When the explanation was given by Cubitt it seemed important in the interest of the prisoner. Cubitt said that when he gave O'Donnell the portrait, he said, "I'll shoot him." To be of use to the Crown that statement would have to be shown to have been made deliberately. But did it so present itself to Cubitt? On the contrary, he took it to be an expression of idle bravado, uttered while the man was laughing, and upon his oath he has told you he attached no importance to it. It was against human experience that a man should form a deliberate attempt to murder and talk about it. The act was not premeditated, but arose from the circumstances described by the prisoner himself. The prisoner would, from his physical infirmities, have been at great disadvantage in any conflict with Carey, and would he have sought such an encounter? Was it not more likely that Carey rushed to his feet when he was called an Irish informer, and drew his pistol, and that O'Donnell being the quicker of the two fired. If Carey had chosen to shoot O'Donnell he could have done so, no doubt, with impunity; but it was enough for the defence that he should show that Carey had the pistol. Carey had the revolver, and under the circumstances there were reasonable grounds for supposing that he would have drawn it. He carried the pistol on shore with him at Madeira, and was it not more likely that he would have taken it with him when he went on shore at the Cape? They had heard that Carey had a revolver pocket, and where was the revolver likely to be but in its place, close at hand and ready for use? The boy had tried to make out that his father did not go ashore on Saturday, but they had it from his mother that he did. They knew further that suspicion had become ascertained fact that Power was Carey, and could they imagine that he did not know it? The people had gathered on the dock side, pointing, and he said to the boy, "Watch those people while I go to the other end of the ship and see whether they are looking at me." James Carey found himself on a vessel with strangers, among men of his own class, with strong feelings, and capable of giving effect to them; and yet they were asked to believe that this was the time he would select for hiding away in a bag the weapon which was his only safeguard and defence. They were told that this man, a conscious coward as he must have been, had put away his weapon in another part of the ship in a bag habitually kept locked, when he had actually taken it ashore with him at Madeira. Could that be true? If it could not be true then they must disregard what he must stigmatize as the lying tale of young Carey that the bag was the receptacle for the revolver, kept ready and fit for immediate use. Thomas Carey said he got the pistol out of the bag. The learned counsel declined to argue whether he went to his father's cabin or not, but they had it from Young that Thomas Carey said that he did, but could not find the revolver, as his father had it.

After adjournment, Mr. Russell, resuming his address, said that he had exhausted all the arguments which occurred to him to press upon the minds of the jury the cardinal point that all the probabilities of the case, strengthened by what James Carey had done before, point to almost the certain conviction that at the Cape he would have had the pistol at hand. It might be said, How was it that no one saw it? and in connection with that it must be remembered that Marks on looking down the skylight could not see the pistol in the hands of O'Donnell. That pistol was bright, while that belonging to Carey was of a dark color, and even less likely to be seen. Although, further, no one saw the pistol on the floor, none of the witnesses say that they could affirm that the pistol was not there. After the firing of the first shot all was confusion, and attention was directed at once to the wounded man, and not to smaller matters. While no one saw the pistol in Carey's hand, it should not be forgotten that no one saw the pistol in the hands of the son, who said he brought it from his mother's berth. It was for the Crown to make out the case, and if they had any doubt as to whether Carey had the pistol, the man's life should not be forfeited to the law. Again, referring to the evidence of young Carey, the learned counsel pointed to his statement with regard to his obtaining the pistol from the bag as most improbable. The bag, he pointed out, contained money and papers, and was habitually kept locked, and it was not likely that it would have been left unlocked on the Sunday. It was not at all improbable that a precocious youth like that might have picked up the pistol with a view to shooting the man who had taken the life of his father, but the opportunity had

passed when O'Donnell was arrested. One of the passengers told
Beecher that young Carey had got a pistol, but when he was searched
by Beecher he denied the possession, and it was not till a second
search was made that it was found in his trousers pocket. The boy
was precocious enough and quick enough to see the importance of
what he was doing, and so he secreted the pistol. He asked the jury
to come to the conclusion that all the probabilities of the case were
against the truth of young Carey's statement, and pointed to the one
conclusion that James Carey would not for a single moment have
trusted himself without that weapon of defence which was given to
him by Inspector Mallon.

The conclusion of Mr. Russell's speech was received with some applause in the gallery, which was instantly suppressed.

His Lordship intimated that any person who again applauded in
that court should be taken into custody.

The Attorney-General, in reply for the Crown, asked the jury, now
that it was admittedly sworn that the prisoner had taken the life of
James Carey, to say that he had taken it without justification.

At this point the prisoner was allowed to retire for a few minutes,
and on his return Justice Denman then directed the jury to convict
the prisoner.

The jury retired at five minutes to seven o'clock to deliberate upon
their verdict, taking with them the bag, the bullets, and two revolvers
that had been referred to in the case.

The Judge, after some time had elapsed, said there was no neces-
sity for the prisoner to remain in court, and he might retire if he
pleased.

O'Donnell said he did not wish to leave the court.

Mr. Justice Denman told him that the jury might possibly be some
time deliberating.

O'Donnell.—Never mind, my Lord, I am as willing to remair as
another.

"Justice" Denman.—Very well.

The jury returned into court at half past seven, having previously
handed a paper to the hanging judge.

The Judge said he found from the paper that had been sent to him that they desired further information upon the question of law affecting the present case. He said that if as honest men they believed that if the prisoner honestly believed he was about to be shot, and with that idea pulled out a pistol and shot the other, this would not be either murder or manslaughter. He asked them where there was any evidence in support of such a suggestion as this in the present case. He reminded them that the evidence proved that three shots had been fired, and that the last shot was in all probability the fatal shot.

The jury then again retired at twenty minutes to eight o'clock.

Mr. Sullivan.—I understood your Lordship to say that the jury must find on the facts proved before them that Carey pointed the pistol at O'Donnell in order to reduce the crime to manslaughter.

The Judge.—Oh, no ; I said nothing of the kind.

Mr. Sullivan.—That they must take the facts proved in—

The Judge.—I certainly told the jury nothing of the kind. I told them nothing as to what they were to find on the facts. It is quite a mistake.

Mr. Sullivan.—I was about to submit to your Lordship that it is not necessary to prove that, and that if they had a reasonable inference they might find justification or manslaughter.

The Judge.—I did not tell them anything to the contrary. I simply asked where was the evidence of it.

Mr. Sullivan thought whether, putting it in that form, it did not come somewhat as a suggestion.

The Judge.—They must have something to justify their verdict, and I have not said a word to the contrary. I do not mean to say anything further. I have placed the case fairly before the jury, and I cannot exhaust every question that the ingenuity of counsel may suggest.

In about three quarters of an hour the jury sent in another paper to the Judge, who directed that they should again come into court.

The Judge having read the paper said he understood that they wished to know what was the meaning of malice aforethought ? His answer was that if one man killed another wilfully the law presumed malice, and the offence was murder, unless circumstances appeared that tended to reduce the crime to manslaughter. In the present case it was said that the offence was not murder, because the deceased had done something which led to violent acts on the part of the prisoner. If they thought this was the case they might convict the prisoner of manslaughter.

A few minutes after the jury had retired a second time they returned into court. Having taken their places in the box their names were called over.

The Clerk.—Do you find the prisoner guilty or not guilty ?

The Foreman.—We find the prisoner guilty.

The prisoner, who had risen from his chair on the entrance of the jury, now folded his arms and surveyed the Judge. On being asked by the Clerk whether he had anything to say before sentence of death was passed upon him, prisoner made no sign, but looked straight before him.

The Judge, who had put on the black cap, then passed sentence of death. He spoke as follows : " Patrick O'Donnell, if I could feel any satisfaction in any part of this case it is the feeling that the jury have not convicted you in haste, that they have taken full time for deliberation, and that they have considered doubts which were even beyond those suggested by the most able and powerful advocate who defended you so ably and so powerfully to-day. The case is one which has not taken you or any one by surprise, because even at the last session of the court application was made on your behalf upon affidavits before me when I sat here on that occasion, intimating that there were persons who might throw further light upon the subject, persons who were said to have been on the ship itself, who could have given further evidence. Ample time was allowed, and no hurry really has taken place from the beginning to the end of the case. You have had as ample an opportunity and as powerful a defence as has ever fallen to the lot of any prisoner to enjoy. And now in the result the jury have come to the conclusion that you did fire that pistol, that you did kill Carey, and that you did it in such circumstances as that you cannot properly or honestly say that you did it in self-defence, or in such a way as to reduce your offence to manslaughter. I cannot say that I disagree with that verdict. I must say that I do not see any reason to disbelieve the evidence of

Cubitt, and that evidence did make it, I think, clear that you were reckless of the life of that man, that you were ready to use a weapon to destroy the life of that wicked, that abominably wicked, man—you did take the life of a dreadfully wicked man. There is no doubt about that. But it would be a most lamentable thing if in this or in any court of justice in a civilized land it could for one moment be laid down that to take the life of a man, wicked though he might be, full of crime, hypocritical and abominable in every way, it can be justifiable for another man to arm himself, or bear arms, with a deadly weapon to kill that man, simply because he was a wicked and abominable man. There would be no civilization, no happiness in this world if such a doctrine as that could for one moment be laid down in a court of justice. It is not so, it is not the law, it is not good, it is dreadful, horrible, to think of, and I fear it is only too plain that you have been induced by bad writings and by advice by people as wicked as Carey himself was to think that it could be justifiable to take the life of a fellow-creature contrary to the law simply because you abominated his wicked deeds, making yourself thereby the executioner of a fellow-creature contrary to the law and in violation of every right principle. It is certain that it cannot be permitted in any civilized country for it to be for one moment doubtful that is what ought to be laid down. The jury have found in your case that you did purposely take the life of that man, and I cannot doubt with what object. I do not say these things for the purpose of hurting your feelings now. I trust you will repent toward God before you die. But in order that it may be thoroughly under- · stood what peril and misery are brought upon people who allow themselves to be led into horrible doctrines of this kind, I have now to pass sentence upon you. The sentence of the court is that you be taken hence to the place whence you came, and thence to a lawful place of execution, there to be hanged by the neck until you be dead, and may God have mercy upon your soul."

As his Lordship concluded, the chaplain of Newgate, who was standing on the bench, said "Amen."

When the officials went to remove the prisoner he shook them aside and said, "Wait a minute ; can I speak?"

The Judge.—No ; it is too late now.

The officials again took hold of O'Donnell to conduct him from the dock, when he became very violent, and roughly shaking them away he exclaimed in a loud voice : "Three cheers for Ireland ! Good-by, United States ! To hell with the bloody British Government and the perjurers who found me guilty !"

As he was borne away he exclaimed, " My death will be avenged !" Then followed the noise of scuffling, the prisoner crying out, " Hold on ; it's a plot made up to destroy me."

The warders dragged him away after a further struggle on the stairs, and his angry protestations continued to be heard by those in court until the doors of the passage underneath were closed.

From the time of his conviction Patrick O'Donnell was kept a close prisoner at Newgate. Prior to his execution he was visited by his wife and brother, and, to the surprise of his warders, he conversed with the latter in his native tongue. He was visited often by the Rev. Father Fleming of the Catholic Chapel at Moorfields. He retired at a reasonable hour on December 16th, the night before his execution, and at a little before six o'clock on that morning he was aroused by his keepers. His health was then good, and he was firm and determined to face his enemies like the brave man he was. About six o'clock the Rev. Mr. Fleming visited him, and breakfast having been served O'Donnell made a hearty meal. He subsequently joined in prayer with the priest, who remained in attendance upon him, offering such consolation as was in his province until the last.

Shortly before eight o'clock Binns commenced to pinion O'Donnell, he submitting to the operation without uttering a word or manifesting any particular emotion. In fact, he exhibited the greatest firmness, and for a moment a smile lighted up his face while the work of buckling the pinion straps was being performed by the executioner. Meanwhile the bell of St. Sepulchre's Church was distinctly heard, and about the same time the prison bell commenced to toll, the scene being one of great solemnity.

Just before the stroke of eight was reached the signal was given, and the preliminary work of the hangman having been completed the procession was formed. First walked a couple of warders, then

O'Donnell, with whom was his spiritual adviser, who was engaged in a prayer, and then the executioner, the rear being brought up by the governor and other officials of the prison, the sheriffs, and under-sheriffs, and several warders. In this order the procession passed out of the prison door along a short, narrow corridor cut off from the rest of the yard by iron railings, and O'Donnell was placed on the scaffold. He walked with a firm and elastic step, and was unassisted in any way by the warders. His head was bare and his shirt collar unfastened. He wore a navy blue suit, a scarlet check shirt, and spring-side boots.

On reaching the drop O'Donnell was at once put into position, and looked calmly around him for a moment, and a smile passed over his face, while his lips moved as though following the exhortations and prayers of the priest. It was remarked that O'Donnell's appearance had somewhat altered since his trial. He looked very pale, and, in addition to short whiskers, wore a short stubble beard, which had been allowed to grow since his condemnation. There had been some anticipation that he would endeavor to make a statement when on the scaffold, but if he ever entertained any such idea he relinquished it, for throughout the fearful ordeal he never uttered a word. Binns performed his work with the utmost despatch. Having got the Irish-American into the proper position, he at once strapped his legs, placed the white cap over his face in another instant, and adjusted the rope round O'Donnell's neck, placing the eye of the noose on the left side of the neck. O'Donnell was a tall man, nearly six feet high, and the executioner had arranged for a fall of eight feet.

Precisely as the clock was striking eight the signal was given to Binns, who immediately stepped back, drew the lever, and the drop fell with a loud crash, which might have been heard a considerable distance. At the same moment the black flag was run up the flagstaff and announced to the anxious crowd outside that "English law" had been carried out, the murmuring of the crowd being distinctly heard within the prison. O'Donnell appeared to die instantly, and according to the statement of the prison surgeon, who watched the execution very closely, there was not even the slightest muscular twitching of any part of the body. An examination of the body showed that the neck was completely broken, so that it is clear that death must have been absolutely painless. The body was allowed to hang for the customary hour, and it was then cut down and placed in a rough shell of considerable depth and width, and of an oblong shape.

After the jury returned the usual verdict, O'Donnell's body was buried in quicklime within the precincts of the prison.

Just as the black flag was raised, O'Donnell's brother stood bareheaded in the door of the Old Bailey, opposite the prison walls. When the flag was run up the pole he exclaimed, " My brother died as bravely as any man ever died." He died an Irishman, and by British decrees an Invincible, and by so doing explained to the world what a farce English law is.

Patrick O'Donnell never made a confession, and the story to that effect was gotten up by the British Government to justify the hanging. The following letter will be found interesting :

" PATRICK FORD, *Editor Irish World*—DEAR SIR : How inadequate are my words to express the heavy debt of gratitude, which shall ever be mine, to *The Irish World*, and the patriotic men of that great and free country, who have so cheerfully responded to the call made by you for my brother's defence.

" Oh, I should exhaust the vocabulary ten times over, were I capable of doing so, before I could reveal to your generous nation the sentiments of my heart ; and now in my brother's name (which was almost the last thing he desired me to do), I return you, one and all, my untold thanks for your noble exertions in his cause ; and to repeat here my brother's last words to me, which was on Saturday before his execution, within the precincts of unhallowed Newgate, and which I also heartily indorse : ' God save Ireland and prosper the United States !'

" In one respect I suppose my brother's conviction took you all by surprise ; and, on the other hand, I suppose you apprehended what the result would be, once he placed his foot on English soil. He was defended by the ablest counsel at the bar. For eloquence, versatility of genius, solidity of erudition, nothing could exceed their efforts in his behalf. But, of course, it availed nothing. As Robert Emmet truly said, they might as well dispense with the ceremony of a trial, for nothing could alter their predetermination to hang him.

"Even before my brother had landed in England, on his voyage from Africa, he was convicted by some of the English journals. These papers were prophetic, as their *decisions* are now fully realized. The subsequent exertions of counsel to have him respited proved ineffectual. Woe betide the unfortunate Irishman who falls into the inhuman hands of those English ! His fate is forever sealed.

"The sympathy felt for my brother appears to have spread all over the continent of Europe. Great Frenchmen and others appealed in vain for him. The English were determined to imbrue their hands in his blood. But he is not the first they murdered. There is a glorious array of Irish martyrs before him whose names will be household words when England's mercenaries, high and low, shall be forgotten, or be remembered only to be detested.

"I visited Patrick at Newgate twice after his conviction, and his resignation and fortitude under the circumstances were marvellous. He himself never for a moment expected a suspension of the sentence. My brother also told me that the officials used to tamper with him in Millbank, but all their artifices would elicit nothing from him.

"He was always exhorting me to bear the coming ordeal with firmness and composure. He never shrank the least, not even on his passage from the cell to the scaffold. Whenever I mentioned to him the strenuous efforts the Americans made to have him get at least 'a fair trial,' and if possible acquitted, he appeared a little moved, which was the only time he betrayed any symptoms of the kind. He knew he would hang, and he said his sacrifice might be an incentive to arouse the Irish to a sense of their duty.

"My brother's last words on this earth were spoken in response to a question put to him by the callous hangman, who asked him if he was being hurt during the process of pinioning. He only smiled and said, 'Go on and finish it !' In a few moments he passed the 'bourn from whence no traveller returneth.'

"Again, in my brother's name, Mr. Ford, and all who have been instrumental in advocating his cause, I return you a thousand, thousand thanks.

"I am, dear sir, forever your obedient servant,

"DANIEL O'DONNELL.

"LETTERKENNY, CO. DONEGAL."

On the same day that O'Donnell was hanged General Roger A. Pryor, who was present at the trial, arrived in New York from London. In reply to the question, "Do you think O'Donnell had a fair trial?" General Pryor said : "As to the summing up of the judge I have no criticism to make. His answer to the inquiry of the jury—the A. B. proposition, as they call it over there—was utterly fatal to any possible hope of the man's acquittal, or conviction of manslaughter even, because in effect and in the most emphatic terms the judge said there was no evidence to justify it. In replying to the jury's question he propounded correctly enough the theory of manslaughter and self-defence, but with a deadly effect he said, ' Gentlemen of the jury, but where is the evidence ? '—meaning by that interrogatory in the strongest terms to negative the idea that there was a particle of evidence looking either to manslaughter or self-defence, thus, in my opinion, usurping the province of the jury, with whom alone it should have been to say whether or not there was evidence of manslaughter or self-defence. I remarked to bystanders at the moment he uttered those words, ' He has put the halter around O'Donnell's neck,' and well he knew it himself, for not long after he left the bench, retired into his private room, and came back with the black cap in his hand. I mean no imputation upon the judge. My notion is that, believing O'Donnell to be guilty of murder, he meant to see that he was convicted. He supposed that his summing up would effect the object, but finding that the jury inclined against a conviction of murder he then delivered the charge which I have criticised."

The assertion that Patrick O'Donnell was not a naturalized citizen of the United States was made by emissaries of the British Government in America for the purpose of allaying popular indignation. O'Donnell was a citizen of the United States, and the following is a true copy of his naturalization certificate at present in the possession of the Secretary of State at Washington, D. C. :

MINOR'S CERTIFICATE OF CITIZENSHIP.

UNITED STATES OF AMERICA,
THE STATE OF OHIO :

Lawrence County Probate Court.

Be it remembered that at a session of the pro-[*mutilated*] in and for said county, held at the court-house at Ironton, on the 6th day of November, A.D. 1876, before George W. Thompson, sole judge of said court, personally came Patrick O'Donnel, a native of Ireland, who came into the United States when under the age of eighteen years, and declared his intention to become a citizen of the United States of America, before the said court, agreeable to the act of Congress in such case made and provided, and proved his residence and character by the oath of Michael McGinley and Hugh Dugan, and being admitted to citizenship by this court, took the oath to support the Constitution of the United States of America, and that he did absolutely and entirely forever renounce and abjure all allegiance and fidelity to every foreign prince, potentate, state, or sovereignty whatsoever, and particularly to the Queen of Great Britain and Ireland.

This is therefore to certify that the said Patrick O'Donnel has complied with the laws of the United States, in such case made and provided, and is therefore admitted a citizen of the United States.

In testimony whereof I have hereun-[*mutilated*] signature and the seal of said probate court, at Ironton, Ohio, this 6th day of November, A.D. 1876.

GEORGE W. THOMPSON,
Probate Judge and ex-officio Clerk.

(Indorsement on back of certificate :) Minor's certificate of citizenship. Probate Court of Lawrence County. Issued 6th November, 1876, to Patrick O'Donnel.

An immense concourse of peasantry assembled on January 24th, 1884, at Derrybeg, County Donegal, birthplace of Patrick O'Donnell, the slayer of James Carey, and assisted in the celebration of mass for the repose of the soul of O'Donnell.   After the mass a mock funeral was held and a coffin was placed in the O'Donnell family burying plot, the people kneeling in prayer around the grave.   Wreaths of immortelles were placed upon the coffin, upon which was the inscription :

Sacred to the Memory of
PATRICK O'DONNELL,
EXECUTED AT LONDON,
Seventeenth of December,
1883.

Thirty-five pounds sterling were subscribed toward a fund to erect a monument to O'Donnell.   A resolution was passed thanking Americans for their assistance and Mr. Victor Hugo for his advocacy of the cause of Ireland.

THE PACKED JURY SYSTEM.

"By hook or by crook" the British Government was determined from the start to convict and hang all Irishmen suspected of being connected with the Invincible Society, for the removal of the tyrants —Burke and Cavendish. Just to what extent it went to effect this measure can be seen by a review of the juries on the Phœnix Park and the Juror Field affairs, and the charges under the Crimes Act preferred against various parties.

The analysis was made by an Irishman, at present the occupant of an English prison. Its sting was in its accuracy and truth. A few of its little ugly notes pointed out the religion, the calling, the political predilection, the dishonest character of the juror, and stamped the list as an exact reflex of the mind of the crown solicitor. There were Archbalds and Beattys, Bloods and Careys, Dockrells and Evanses, Findlaters and Gibsons, Griffiths and Harrises, Johnsons and Joneses, Keoghs and Leeches, Macnies and Nuzums, Ogilvies and Phillipses, Robertses and Shankses, Townsends and Wardrops, a motley crew of as obliging men as ever begged a ticket for themselves and their wives to be admitted to a Castle ball.

In giving the names and summing up the analysis of the Phœnix Park and Field cases the writer says : " Of the juries that convicted, the overwhelming majority were landlords, agents, magistrates, shop-keepers, or persons directly connected or beholden to Castle or landlord interests. Thirteen served twice, five three times, one four times. Of the total sixty-two were Protestants and twenty-two Catholics—the latter, without exception, being of the anti-National stripe." Continuing the analysis in the eighteen other trials, showing how many times each juror served and the extent to which these juries were packed, the writer says :

" The reader will be at once struck by the frequent recurrence of the same names, so frequent as to give to some gentlemen the appearance of being special jurors by profession. The recurrence is not to be accounted for, as might be supposed, by the exhaustion of the names on the panels, as each commission had two special panels of one hundred names each struck for itself, and the greatest number of trials on any commission was on the first, where there were thirteen, eleven convictions and two disagreements.   We have shown that on this commission there were for eleven trials seventeen jurors who served twice, and three jurors who served three times.   If a fresh jury had been called for each trial one hundred and thirty-two jurors out of the two hundred on the panels would have served, instead of only one hundred and nine, the same men being put on again and again by the Crown, while ninety-one fresh jurors were still available. On the second commission for five trials, ten jurors served twice, thus reducing the proper number from sixty to fifty, while one hundred and fifty were still available.   On the third commission this peculiarity is most striking ; for five trials, seven jurors served twice, and three served three times, reducing the proper number of jurors from sixty to forty-seven, while one hundred and fifty-three were still available.   The effect of these figures would be increased if the juries which failed to agree on a verdict were also analyzed, as most of the jurors who served on these served again on trials where convictions were obtained, some of the jurors whose names are contained in this publication having actually served four times.   On Patrick Walsh's first trial, which resulted in a disagreement, all the jurors, except one, had served or did afterward serve on trials which resulted in convictions ; three of them—William Gibson, 14 Lower Ormonde Quay, W. James Halliday, Brookville, Monkstown, and John B. Johnston, 8 Clyde Road—having served in all three times, and one, Francis Johnston, Accountant-General of the Bank of Ireland, having served four times.   In addition one juror who served twice during the first commission served a third time on the second.   One juror who served once on the first commission served also on the second, and one who served on the second commission served again on the third.   Thus instead of two hundred and sixteen jurors for eighteen prisoners, only one hundred and sixty-seven officiated out of eight hundred on the panels.

" During the four commissions only one prisoner was acquitted, on the fourth. To those who are at all familiar with the City and County of Dublin it will not be necessary to point out how exclusively these jurors were drawn from the class that is most hostile to the great bulk of the people, and from those traders who are most dependent on that class for their livelihood.

" It is interesting to note that the Secretary of the Dublin Property Defei ze Association was placed on the first capital trial, and to recollect that, at a recent trial of some agents of the Property Defence Association for Whiteboyism, in the County Limerick, the Crown stated that no person who had been a member of the Land League would be allowed to serve on the jury, as an impartial jury could not otherwise be secured. A cynic might inquire why the Crown does not order all members of the Property Defence Association to stand aside when a Land Leaguer is on his trial."

THE EFFECT OF THE EXECUTIONS.

Dr. Hamilton Williams, when spoken to on the subject of the removals of Cavendish and Burke, upheld the action of the patriots, and said :

" The effect of the execution of Cavendish and Burke was to save us from our friends in England. Mr. Parnell is a parliamentarian and wedded to parliamentary methods. The treaty of Kilmainham, so called, if carried into execution, would have done for the farmers and the smaller tradesmen in Ireland what the concession of Catholic emancipation did for the high or middle Catholic class. It would have cut them off from the National ranks. The great object, in fact the sole object, of the men who look to the well-being of Ireland is complete separation of the two countries. Possibly from a board-of-trade standpoint that separation would act injuriously to Ireland, but we want to restore to Ireland her separate standing as a nation and a people, cost what it may. Ireland, though a small country, has a great future before her ; not a future like Germany or Russia, with their large populations and their lust of territory. Ireland is destined to be again a great intellectual centre for Europe."

THE END.

COOGAN BROTHERS,

121, 123, 125, 127 Bowery, cor. Grand St.,

NEW YORK,

MANUFACTURERS OF

Parlor, Library, and

Chamber

FURNITURE.

Their Retail Warerooms are the largest in the United States,

COVERING OVER

R. M. Walters'

PIANOS,

57 & 59 University Place,

COR. E. 12th STREET,

NEW YORK.

The Narvesen Piano manufactured by R. M. Walters is meeting with great success from musicians and the public generally. The late Geu. Grafulla, Bandmaster of the 7th Regiment, used one of these pianos in his house for fifteen years. Mr. Walters keeps a large assortment of new and second-hand pianos always on hand for cash, credit, or rent.

McSWYNY,

Gentlemen's Fine Shoes,

No. 240 BROADWAY, Opposite Post-office, NEW YORK.

WATERPROOF SHOES A SPECIALTY.

First Prize Medal Awarded at American Institute.

JUDGES' REPORT.

BRYAN G. McSWYNY, 240 BROADWAY.
Neat and artistic in design, good material, workmanship excellent in every respect. The Waterproof material unsurpassed.
We recommend a Medal of Superiority.   CHAS. WAGNER HULL, Gen'l Sup't.

"NUMBER ONE"

AND THE

IRISH INVINCIBLES.

This book can be obtained by addressing
"NUMBER ONE" PUBLICATION CO.,
P. O. Box No. 1486, NEW YORK CITY.

Single Copies, 25 Cents.   Discount to Dealers.

R D - 1.1.